NATIONAL MARITIME MUSEUM

The last of the SAILING COASTERS

Reminiscences and observations of the days in the Severn trows, coasting ketches and schooners

Edmund Eglinton

London
HER MAJESTY'S STATIONERY OFFICE

Contents

Plates

Map of the Severn Estuary

Introduction

I have been very lucky to know well a number of men who made their livings from merchant sailing vessels in their last years. To mention a few, William Lamey, Master and owner of the ketch *Hobah* was a boyhood friend. From Bill Shiller of the ketch *Lively* I learned the elements of boat handling and I sailed to the Baltic with Ivar Hägerstrand, the last man save one to command a laden merchant sailing ship on passage round Cape Horn. Captain W J Slade, with over forty years in sail behind him, has been a friend and collaborator for nearly 30 years. From Karl V Karlsson, Master of the four-masted schooner *Atlas*, I have learned a great deal about the real life in merchant sailing vessels.

In the normal course it seemed unlikely that there would be fresh acquaintance of this kind. But in 1977 I received a letter from a man who said that he had read in 'West Country Coasting Ketches', which Captain W J Slade and I wrote together, of my recollection of being taken at the age of 6 to see the wreck of the ketch *Thomasine & Mary* on the north Somerset coast near Portishead. The writer said that he had been one of the crew of two of the vessel when she was lost. The request for an account of the casualty brought a brief, lucid narrative (now incorporated in this volume). The long arm of coincidence stretched out further when a visit to Edmund Eglinton revealed that he once owned the house to which I was taken (in a pony and trap) from the nursing home in the nearby town where I was born.

A result of this new acquaintance is this splendid book of unique and detailed reminiscence of a part of the British coasting trade in sailing vessels not recorded before. The local trade of the Severn and Bristol Channel in trows and ketches was a very skilled business, calling for very high standards of shiphandling and most intimate local knowledge. Here something of it is recorded at first hand, so vividly that the story can scarcely fail to fascinate anyone interested in the sorts of lives which people lived in that utterly remote world before, during, and shortly after the great divide of the First World War. I am very glad indeed that this book has been written and that through Edmund Eglinton the whole little maritime world that was in danger of being lost now has some record.

Basil Greenhill
DIRECTOR
NATIONAL MARITIME MUSEUM
Greenwich, 1980

Acknowledgements

To those who may enjoy reading this simple account of the kind of life it was in the now extinct Severn trows, and the coastal ketches and schooners during the early part of this century must thank, not I who wrote the manuscript, but Dr Basil Greenhill CMG, Director of the National Maritime Museum, who, after reading a very short account – written by me at his request – of the loss of a vessel I was in, prevailed upon me to enlarge upon it, and later to write a fuller account from my earliest memories.

Dr Greenhill's vast knowledge and unbounded enthusiasm concerning the era of sail, and the many kinds of sailing vessels that ranged the near and distant seas – their only power the wind – rekindled in myself a flame that had never really died, bringing to the writing of the words much joy and satisfaction in my recollection.

Edmund Eglinton
'Landfall' Bleadon 1980

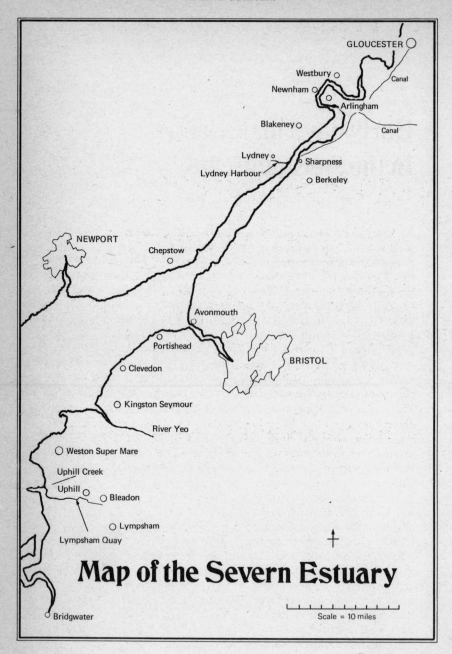

GLOUCESTER

Canal

Westbury

Newnham

Arlingham

Blakeney

Canal

Lydney

Sharpness

Lydney Harbour

Berkeley

NEWPORT

Chepstow

Avonmouth

Portishead

BRISTOL

Clevedon

Kingston Seymour

River Yeo

Weston Super Mare

Uphill Creek

Uphill

Bleadon

Lympsham

Lympsham Quay

Map of the Severn Estuary

Scale = 10 miles

Bridgwater

Early days in the trows in the Severn Estuary

As I was not fortunate enough to be born in a seaport or harbour from whence so many small sailing vessels traded in the early twentieth century, I must have been about eight years old before I set foot aboard one of them. But I was born less than a mile from the sea on the Somerset coast, and only about half a mile from the banks of the River Yeo. In *The Merchant Schooners*, volume 1, by Basil Greenhill, I saw the river referred to as the 'Congresbury Yeo'. I cannot recall it being called by that name, but it certainly flows through Congresbury and the name is appropriate.

At that time my father was engaged in the construction of the sea walls that were being built in an attempt to halt the inroad of the sea along that stretch of shore. He spent the latter half of his life in that very frustrating battle. As far as I can recall it, it was about the year 1910 that a little vessel was purchased to transport the walling stone for those walls from Wains Hill Quarry further up the coast to the sites on our foreshore. The little ship was what was then termed a stump-masted open trow with side cloths; her name was the *Providence* and she was smack rigged.

My father, who was the contractor on the construction work, had spent much of his early life in the trows and was himself in charge of the *Providence*. I do not recollect the 'whys and where-fores' of the arrangement but I have very vivid recollections of what my sister Edith and I had to do. The masons working on the walls had built a stack of dry driftwood on top of a heap of straw and covered it to keep it dry. My sister and I had to be on the foreshore two hours before high water and had been directed to keep a sharp lookout for a white light being dipped to seaward. This we did, but it was a very dark and lonely shore and, waiting there in the darkness with the eerie lapping of the water as the rising tide came running and gurgling in over the mud flats, and the plaintive cries of the curlew, the mallards and the gulls being driven inland, we were indeed fearful and trembling, but we crouched low beside the unlit beacon and watched. Then the light appeared! A tiny light, it seemed so very far away (it was probably two to three miles) showing for a few seconds, then concealed below the bulwarks and lifted again to show its welcome beam – a dipping light, our signal from our father's vessel. Our courage returned and we both frantically fumbled for the matches to set the beacon alight. The straw caught, then the twigs, and soon the flames were roaring and leaping high aloft. We felt wild with joy, and relief at the comfort of the fire. Later we saw a red light which seemed far out to sea (I did not know then that this was her port navigation light). Then with mounting excitement, we suddenly saw a vivid green light – the *Providence* had gone about and was coming in, with the now ebb tide sweeping her down, on the starboard tack. We kept throwing on more wood, quite needlessly, and both frantically jumping up and down; my sister was only 15 years of age.

Suddenly, as the little vessel sailed into the range of the firelight, we saw the reflection of the flames from her dripping bows, then the faint outline of her sails against the sombre background of the sky, and simultaneously came the raucous shouts of the men, then the creaking of the blocks and the rasping of the hanks on the wire stays as the jibs came down. Then came the roar of the anchor chain as it ran out of the hawse pipe. The *Providence* was now only about 60 feet from the shore and we could see the tracery of her rigging and cordage outlined against the sky. A sight never to be forgotten – a picture of a little ship sailing in out of the darkness into the limited lighting of the flames of our beacon, seeming to float on liquid silver. Now, nearly 70 years later, this picture comes to me as vividly as on that very momentous occasion, an occasion of heart-thumping excitement and great joy. My father called out to us to hurry home to 'tell mother he had arrived safely'. I evidently fell asleep at the supper table that night and my mother, I was told, carried me up to bed.

The next morning the race to the shore! It had not been a dream! There was the *Providence* moored 'all fours' with two stream anchors out from her port and starboard quarters, and two heavy warps to stakes on shore. The crew were manning the dolly winch and 'bearing off' the tubs of stone as they were hoisted out of the hold of the vessel. The 'bearing off' man stood on a gang-plank which was rigged athwart the ship with the end jutting well clear of the side where the stone was to be tipped. As the tub of stone was whipped up from the hold he would grab the tub as the winch men held it about four feet above the plank, then push and run with it to the end of the gang plank shouting 'lower' as he neared the end so that the tub would usually land exactly on the end of the gangplank where it could be tipped easily over the side. Meantime another tub was being loaded by the men in the hold and, as the empty one came back, the full one would be hooked on and hoisted away aloft. All this was hard and monotonous work, urgent work, for the vessel had to be away on the next tide; should a strong wind come to blow directly on the shore, or even at a slant, there would be small chance of getting her away without damage or even becoming a total loss. It was certainly always a most anxious time for the master. Everyone concerned knew this and accepted the need for haste in such a situation. No trade unions were there to decree that the stone masons should not become stevedores. No dissenters to curb the will of willing men to happily do all in their power to set the vessel free from that dangerous shore.

The tubs used for unloading the stone were an innovation for that particular commodity. When a vessel was discharging coal and was using her own gear baskets were used, but baskets would not stand up to the heavy walling stone, some of which weighed over a hundredweight.

But I knew nothing of these things on that day in 1910. One of the men carried me out to the *Providence* over the mud and put me on a ladder to enable me to climb on board. Here was one of the scores of vessels that every week could be seen sailing up and down past our coast, but the first I had ever been aboard. The wonder of it all! Everything seemed so huge, so heavy, and so mighty; my arms would not encircle the mast. Then the mass of ropes big and small and chain and wire. The canvas of the sails, the like which I had observed so many times shaking in the wind as the vessels off our shore went about, and appeared to be like silken curtains trembling in a breeze, proved to be so thick and tough that I could not even bend a single fold with my puny little hands. Then the smell! Everywhere I went, on deck or below, it was there, not an objectionable odour, yet one that took some getting used to. I knew afterwards that the smell was a combination of odours from Stockholm tar, oakum, pitch and all kinds of rope and twines containing tar and maybe creosote. Not only did it pervade the whole ship but one's clothes were soon impregnated; yet after 24 hours aboard it was hardly noticeable, but this, of course, I only discovered much later on.

During the morning ''lowance time' (allowance time) or tea break, as it is called today, my father took me down to his cabin. This was another spellbinding occasion, for, although I cannot recall much about the cabin itself, I vividly remember the gleaming brass lamp with a tall glass chimney which swung on gimbals supported by a bracket from the side panelling. Then there was the shelf with a shining brass rail that swept in a lovely curve around the after end of the cabin, and a small square black range on which stood the steaming kettle. The deck hand came down and made some tea by the simple method of throwing a handful of tea direct into the boiling water in the kettle. Then the mate came down and the four of us had tea and biscuits together, tea which came straight from the kettle and biscuits that had to be soaked. It was not often one saw a teapot in the trows those days – it just wasn't the thing! Here indeed was real life, drinking tea in a ship's cabin with the crew, listening to the nautical phraseology and the predictions of the weather whilst the mate loaded my tea with Nestlé's condensed milk. I must have grown two inches during those few minutes. That day I caught that incurable malady, the love of ships and sails and the smell of oakum. I have it still after nigh on 70 years.

After a few cargoes the *Providence* was lost. Evidently she was old and ripe, and the grounding on the hard berths near the quarry was more than her bottom could withstand. She sprang some butts off Clevedon and sank within a few minutes. My father's gunmetal watch which became full of sea water when they scrabbled off the deck into the boat hung over our mantelpiece for many years as a reminder of that unfortunate night – the time by it showed 9.45.

The next vessel to bring stone to the Kingston Seymour walls was the little *Nellie*, another stump-masted open trow. She was owned and skippered by Capt W Rowles of Clevedon. In the last quarter of the 19th century Capt Rowles and his brother John owned two deck trows, the *William and Martha* and the *Brothers*. My father had sailed with them in both those vessels and he and Capt Rowles were friends.

The Rowles had a motorboat at Clevedon used for fishing in the winter and pleasure trips in the summer. This was very useful for, should the wind come in from the north west whilst the *Nellie* was discharging the boat could be sent down to help get her clear of the breakers from which the trow when light had to depend on her stern anchors and then kedges to warp her clear of the surf before sail could be set to try to claw her clear of the lee shore. If the wind proved to be too northerly she could be helped back into the river Yeo and there lie secure waiting for a slant to get her clear of the shore.

Then came the 1914 war. In the spring of 1916 I left the village school to go to work on the sea walls. I was allowed to leave because men were now scarce and the sea defence work was considered important. But stone for the walls was getting used up, there being no vessels available to bring it to our coast.

With the end of the war my father ordered some stone from Chepstow (I believe the Clevedon quarry was at that time closed). It was difficult to get owners to risk their vessels on an open shore and before agreement was reached the captain and owner of the trow *Palace*, Capt Simms, came to see the mooring and berthing arrangements. Then came the morning when the *Palace* appeared off our shore and I was overjoyed to see she was ketch rigged. With her sails, some white, some tanned, all set and drawing, including a huge square-headed gaff topsail and three jibs, she looked to me so lofty and stately, gliding along seemingly without effort, swelling in size as she slipped nearer in, her wet weather side glistening in the morning sun. Suddenly a shout 'Ease up' came across the water. I knew this meant the vessel was to be put on the opposite tack. With the easing of the jib sheets, spilling the wind out of those headsails the canvas shook and slammed with noise like pistol shots. Then, as the ship came nearly head to wind, the canvas of the mainsail joined in the fun, thrashing and rumbling like thunder, but not for many seconds; one last crashing sound as the main boom, and then the mizzen boom, slid over to leeward and all was quiet again. Now on the starboard tack with the ebb tide under her lee bow keeping her up to windward she edged in to the shore; the crew could see the marker poles now, and the pole in the water near the berth with a cross-bar showing whatever depth was required for that particular vessel.

We (for the masons and some others had gathered by now) saw the topsail suddenly come down, then the flying jib and the boom jib as she neared the berth; we heard the master calling for the main peak to be lowered and the main tack to be hoisted (this was known as scandalising the mainsail). The tide was now sending her astern whilst at the same time she was being sheered in towards the berth. Next came the shout to stand by to let go the anchor, a few seconds later 'let go', then 'pay out the chain'. Capt Simms (for he it was) had neatly and skilfully put his vessel nearly into her berth and at the same time left his anchor some 30 fathoms off ready for heaving the ship off from her berth when she floated on the evening tide.

The vessel's boat then brought a warp ashore from the starboard bow and with it leading to the dolly winch, the *Palace* was hove exactly in place in her berth. But conditions for this manoeuvre had to be just right – for instance, a big tide giving plenty of water.

The old *Palace* did not look so good when viewed at close quarters; lacking in paint, shabby and bluff bowed. But one feature that struck me was her long bowsprit, it looked nearly half as long as the ship. But this I later discovered was common in those vessels. My father explained to me that the jibs that 'stuck out so far ahead' had great pulling power. In later years I proved this to be true.

I helped to discharge the *Palace*; my first job was on board a vessel. I was down in the hold loading the stone into the tubs. Being an open trow, the first 10 or 15 tons could be lifted and thrown directly over the side, but as the level got lower the tubs had to be used. The heaviest stones – some well over a hundred-weight – had to be lowered carefully into the tubs otherwise the tubs, which were only beer barrels sawn in half, with holes drilled for chains that acted as slings, would quickly be smashed to pieces.

With the coming of the evening tide the old *Palace* floated and, as she lifted, the heap of stones which had built up against her side as high, or higher than her gunwale, pushed the vessel aside and went rumbling down to form a perfectly rounded heap on the mud not many paces from where they had to be used. I helped heave the anchor chain in to get the ship off to her anchor. Then gave a hand to hoist the mainsail and mizzen; they then put me ashore in the boat and, with the wind off-shore, the anchor was quickly hove up, the headsails set, the *Palace* slipped away into the night.

The next spring tides the *Palace* arrived again. But although it was a fine morning there was a bit of a swell so that there was some difficulty in holding the vessel in the berth prepared for her. A bowrope parted caused by a back surge of the swell, but a second warp was quickly ferried in by the ship's boat. I flung a heaving line to the plunging boat and, with that, hauled the warp ashore. It was a four-inch coir (grass rope) and, most unusual, there was no bowline in it, neither did I have time to make one as the vessel was surging away from the berth and I had not a second to lose, otherwise the warp would not reach the mooring post – a four-inch stake driven into the ground. I just managed to take two turns around the stake and by putting both feet against it and hanging on to the end of the warp, hoped to keep it from surging (slipping) around the stake. I certainly managed to prevent this, but I could see the warp stretching down to half its size. It did not part; instead the four-inch oaken stake sheered off level with the ground and, as I was right in front of it, the warp, acting like a giant piece of elastic, whipped the stake through the air like a bullet. It struck me full in the face and flung me about ten feet. I have the scars to this day and never after did I stand the fore side of a mooring post! The *Palace* now was right away from her berth and, the tide ebbing, had to wait until next day to discharge.

I never saw the *Palace* again after that episode. The next trow to bring stone from Chepstow was the little stump master, the *Success*. She was much smaller than the *Palace* and drew much less water. She also belonged to the Simms family. I could have had a job in either of these vessels, but my father wanted me on the walls. Cement in those days came in 200lb jute sacks and I was able, young as I was, to carry these up the steep sea bank! But those little vessels had infected me with such a fever that I lived only for the day when one would become my floating home.

Then came the day when I saw my father talking to a man in a reefer jacket and peaked nautical cap. Moreover he had golden earrings and a white moutache, which seemed to accentuate the healthy red of his weather-beaten face. He had a deep voice and a ready tongue and the first words I heard him say were, 'Yes, Tom, I'll put 'um anywhere you want 'um, providing there's water enough, for ten shillings a ton.' This man was Capt Leonard Smart and he was part owner of the little ketch *Jane*. Capt Smart lived in Uphill on the river Axe in Somerset. The other part owner was the local coal merchant of Uphill and his name was Hart.

Later my father told me that he had reached agreement with Capt Smart to bring good walling stone from Uphill Quarry to the Kingston Seymour walls for 10/- per ton. The crew of the *Jane* was to use the ship's gear to unload, but my father agreed to put three men in the hold to fill the tubs. The little *Jane* was a flush deck trow of 80 tons burden, so three men were needed in the hold because the tubs of stone had to be dragged out to the area directly below the hatchway, which was not necessary in the hold of an open trow. Came the day when the *Jane* was loaded and ready to leave the River Axe for her first cargo to the Kingston walls. It was a very low spring tide, however, and as the tides were also cutting, it was arranged for my father to be aboard for the first trip, as there would be barely enough water at the highest moment of the tide to accommodate the vessel in the berth. So the *Jane*, to save time, actually had to be sailed into the mud berth and 'dumpted' as Capt Smart termed it, and her anchors carried off after the tide had ebbed. Of course, my father took me with him, for I already had quite a lot of experience in mooring the various trows, and the

heavy 'anchor drill' that went with it. I was conversant also with
the hoisting and the furling of the sails. But this was my first trip!
The first time ever in a vessel under sail from one place to another!

It was only a few miles but I was thrilled beyond measure. I
recall it was a lovely fine morning when we sailed out of the Axe
– it had to be to enable the captain to carry out the beaching that
was intended. But I recall little else of the trip except the great
excitement of the arrival off our foreshore. We were early and
sailing in within about three cable lengths of the walls we could see
the marker pole in the water with the cross bar (showing the depth
of water required) well clear of the surface. We were too early, so
the vessel was put about and stood off the shore for about ten
minutes, the topsail meantime being taken in. The tide was now
easing, we were not being swept too far above the berth. The
skipper now put the vessel about again ready for the 'run in'. My
father was in the bows with the binoculars, the mate and myself
were ordered to stand by the main halyards ready to lower the
mainsail when the word was given. Then came the orders 'haul
down the jibs' (this to my father), and then 'lower away the mainsail, quickly now'. The skipper meantime had dropped the peak of
the mizzen and hauled up the tack, whilst the *Jane*, suddenly naked
of sail, now about a cable's length from the berth, seemed to me
to be forging ahead too quickly. We could see the cross bar on the
marker pole just clear of the water. Only a length of the ship to go
now and still we slipped ahead through the water! Then an imper-
ceptible rise in the deck beneath one's feet, she had smelt the mud,
the movement slowed, then stopped; we were in the berth, exactly
right, on a bed of soft mud. The captain beamed, everyone breathed
again; the *Jane* had been dumped successfully, and without fuss.
Never did a breakfast of thick rashers of very fat bacon and eggs,
go down so well. Then to work! We had already been over four
hours with plenty to do, but now 80 tons of stone had to be got
over the side before the vessel floated again. But the masons were
waiting to take their place in the hold. Before the transport of the
stone to the walls by the various trows, I remember the stone being
hauled from Yatton with a horse and putt (a two wheeled tip cart)
and the last part of the journey was across three fields, about half
a mile. Each load could not have been more than a ton. The *Jane*'s
cargo therefore of 80 tons represented 80 journeys to the Congresbury boundary of Yatton, a total mileage for the horse of about
750 and, with loading the putt, at least 200 hours work for the man
and horse. Yet here was the *Jane* delivering 80 tons right on the
site for 10/- per ton. Here was real progress!

That evening the *Jane* floated more than an hour before high water. The wind being easterly, there had been no need to take off the heavy stream anchor – or anchors. Instead a kedge had been put out and a small warp was enough to haul the little vessel off clear of her berth. Then setting all sail we sailed down over the tide to St Thomas's Head, then came the ebb and with a fair wind we quickly slipped past Woodspring Point and hauled our wind to cross the Weston Bay. We 'saved our water' into the mouth of the Axe and anchored for the night in what was then known as 'the hole'. My father did not come on the return trip, but I stayed on board for Capt Smart had as mate a man I only knew as Bill. He was an ex-navy man, but did not like going aloft so I was delighted when the captain asked me to go.

That morning I had loosed the topsail aloft when leaving the Axe, tied it up on arrival at the Kingston walls, loosed and furled it again on the return trip, in addition to helping handling all the other sails. Then there was the nine hours hard work loading the tubs in the hold. I crawled into the bunk that night too tired to remove my clothes, too tired to eat or even talk, but full of un-bounded happiness; proud indeed of my great day aboard the *Jane* – a vessel with flush decks from fore to aft, no dodging over a gang-plank, over an open hold as in a side cloth trow. The kind of ship one read about. I was put ashore early the next morning for I had to go home to work on the walls.

When the next cargo was loaded and there was water enough into the sea walls on our foreshore, Capt Smart asked for me to make my second trip in the *Jane*. This time there was a different mate aboard; his name was Walter Radford, but the skipper called him 'Whiskers', though he had no beard. I liked Mr Radford (as I had to call him); he had been 'everywhere' and 'done everything' – including soldiering in India. Capt Smart had been in many smart ships in the Far East trade; he too had been 'everywhere' including around Cape Horn. The tales of their experiences filled me with wonder and I was proud indeed to be shipmates with two such men – with their salty language and the skipper's gold earrings.

On that trip, before we left the river Axe, Capt Smart gave me some practical sculling lessons in the ship's boat. I had to scull a heavy warp ashore and various other exercises, including the correct way to heave a kedge whilst standing clear of the line, and keeping the line clear of the stock of the kedge. 'Always put a boat alongside of a vessel with her bow heading the same way as the ship', he told me, also 'never put your hand on the gunwale of the boat that is towards the ship when boarding, or lying alongside, men had lost their fingers in so doing, and never stand on a thwart when sculling', etc. These things I have never forgotten and always practised. They were never questioned. I was not unaware that the practice with the heavy warp was because it was intended I should be the 'boatman' when we berthed at the Kingston walls.

That trip was quite uneventful. Being young and agile I was the topsail man. I also loosed and tied up the three jibs. I was keen and this was what I loved to do. There çame the day when I went down to join the *Jane* to bring a cargo to the Kingston walls and found she was down in 'the hole' by the mouth of the Axe. Capt Smart came in to the bank of the river to take me off. His first words were a warning not to bring any mud aboard. 'Sit on the gunwale and wash your boots; never forget that!' On arrival on board and not seeing the mate 'Whiskers', the captain informed me 'he's not coming this trip, we'll have to manage.' I then found out that after discharging the stone we were going on to Lydney for a cargo of coal.

Now I had heard so much about the perils of the River Severn from my father, and many others, that the captain's announcement that he and I alone were taking the *Jane* to Lydney caused me some apprehension, but this was somewhat alleviated by the joy of a voyage to different waters.

When it was time to get under way, we hoisted the mainsail and heaved in some of the cable. Then the skipper said, 'Ted, go out and loose your jibs, after that go up and loose your topsail.' My jibs! My topsail! Here was quite a different tone; if it was meant to encourage me it certainly succeeded. Never had I felt more proud – or more tall. But I did not preen myself for long, for in less than an hour the *Jane* was struck by lightning and I was the most frightened boy on earth.

There was a lovely summer breeze off shore that unforgettable morning; we set off about 5.30 am. Immediately we hove the anchor. I hoisted the jibs and the staysail, whilst the skipper took the helm and hoisted the mizzen. After passing the Black Rock he gave me a hand to hoist the topsail and sheet it home. The *Jane* must have looked a picture from the promenade on that lovely morning, running out with everything free. Whilst getting under way we had noticed a black cloud over the Newport area on the Welsh coast which we both thought may be a thunderstorm. When passing Sand Bay, the black cloud seemed to be spreading rapidly over the sky ahead and towards us, although we still had a fair wind. Off Sand Point our fair wind suddenly died and Captain Smart with 'I don't like the look of this', decided to take down the topsail. We quickly hauled it down and, whilst I went aloft to ride it down and secure it with the gasket, the skipper hauled down the flying jib. On returning from aloft I went out and furled the jib; we then took in the boom jib and this I also furled. The cloud had now blotted out the sun and ahead of us to the north west we could see the 'black puffs' racing over the water towards us.

The vessel was now on the starboard tack with her head to seaward. The heavy cloud seemed to come right down to the topmast truck and the atmosphere was most oppressive and heavy. We flattened the standing jib right in with both sheets fast to the bitts, keeping the sail dead in the centre of the vessel. We also hauled up the tack of the mainsail; the mainsail had a loose foot like all the trows, and hauling up the tack was a very speedy way of shortening sail. We were now hove to of course and then, with the becket on the wheel, the captain told me to stand by the main throat halyards whilst he stood by the peak halyards ready to run the mainsail right down should the need arise. The lightning forked down from the cloud in all directions like many coloured curtains, whilst the thunder cracked and rumbled without a pause. The weight of rain, bucketing down as it did, seemed to kill the wind. Then right overhead a vivid red ball of fire burst through the cloud, and simultaneously an explosion like the crack of a mighty naval gun together with a terrific jar through the deck beneath our feet. Sparks and balls of fire seemed to fall on and around the ship. I was petrified with fear, and in the glare of all this fearsome display of mighty force saw the captain's face, uncommonly pale, and full of consternation. 'We've been struck,' he shouted. 'Keep hold of the halyard!' During all the noise and fire there was a terrible smell. 'I can smell burning,' I shouted. 'Shut up!' he called back – but looking around as if it may be true – 'tis sulphur.' But I had never smelt sulphur before.

After this the darkness lifted as the centre of the storm moved farther away. The wind, which had never reached above force 6, eased and came from the eastward. That strange and frightening storm had only stayed with us about an hour, but through life I have never forgotten those awful fireballs and the sulphurous smell. Even now nearly 60 years after, the nearness of a thunderstorm gives me a feeling of apprehension and a desire not to be exposed.

Back to the *Jane*. We were now about three miles off and the tide had taken us above our destination. Putting her on the other tack with all sail again set except the top sail, the east wind quickly took us in across the tide and we berthed with Capt Smart's usual adeptness at highwater. My father, who had been on the lookout, had seen us off Sand Point, had observed the topsail and jibs taken down and then, as he said, 'the cloud seemed to curve down from the sky and cover you like a huge paw'.

Capt Smart felt certain that the lightning had struck the flying jib stay – which is attached to the upper part of the topmast at one end and the spider band on the outer end of the bowsprit the other end. This would then have given the bolt a continuous lead to the chain bobstay and down to the ironwork of the stem and the surface of the sea – a conductor. This would have explained the definite jar we had felt under our feet. But we found no scars, only a scorched patch on the painted end of the bowsprit.

We had been up and about since 4.30 that morning; then the freak storm had taken its toll both mentally and physically. For myself all the bounce of the morning on leaving the river was completely gone; I felt humble. It was a lesson, and a good lesson. But the stone had to be discharged. I was one of the men on the dolly winch and the *Jane* was empty long before high water on the evening tide. My father's men helped us take down the discharging gear and put the beams and hatches on (the hatches were really only planks.) They also helped us set the mainsail. Then with the wind off shore, we set the head sails and were away, for the skipper was anxious to get clear of the open shore and as far as possible towards Portishead with the last of the flood tide. Going aloft to loose the topsail that evening my agility was gone, and I thought of my father going home to a lovely hot supper! We managed to get above Clevedon before the tide came down, and anchored for a blessed few hours' rest. Of course the topsail had to be taken down and tied up, besides the jibs and staysail, but these latter were not furled. Being a fine night the mainsail and mizzen were left up – but with both tacks hauled up. The captain now put some salt cod, which had already been soaked, in the saucepan whilst I peeled some potatoes, and these two commodities, together with plenty of butter and bread, were our supper. By now it was over an hour's ebb; in less than five hours we would be preparing to weigh anchor again, or sooner should a change of wind put us on a lee shore before that. Such was the way of life in the trows.

At 2.30 am the next morning we started to heave in the anchor chain for it was slack water. Before this I had to light the side lights and stand them below the bulwarks ready to be put in their light boards as soon as the anchor light came down. Always being used to long nights' sleep at home the lack of sleep seemed a real punishment, especially when I had to go aloft in the darkness to loose the topsail. With the anchor up and the headsail set, the tacks of the main and mizzen hauled down and 'my topsail' sheeted home, the wind being offshore we were soon off Portishead and the glow of dawn was in the sky. With the wind easterly and on the starboard tack we headed towards that awesome and narrow stretch of water known as 'The Shoots'. That morning, however, with an easterly breeze, good visibility and in daylight, as Capt Smart pointed out, it was all that could be desired. But these were not the words he used! Actually he said, 'We're b . . . . lucky! When the thunderstorm came on us I thought you must be a Jonah!' The English Stones on our starboard side and the Gruggy Rock to port were both visible at that early state of tide. The little *Jane* heeled, and the hum of the wind in the rigging increased as we neared the English Stones. This was the stronger run of tide as we entered the narrows thrusting us up to windward, increasing our speed through the water; and the current, increasing our speed over the ground, made us seem to be racing past the nearby rocks with the speed of a train. Actually I suppose our speed over the ground was a little less than nine miles per hour. Therefore we had passed through the Shoots in about fifteen minutes. To me, on that lovely early morning, it was a delightful and exhilarating experience.

Passing the Charston Rock we hauled in the sheets and put the vessel on the port tack in a 'short leg' to windward and, although our bowsprit was now pointing down towards Bristol, the *Jane* was still being swept up stern first towards our destination at quite a speed. Such is the River Severn!

That morning as we were early, about two miles below Lydney over the Lydney Sands, we had to put the vessel's head down against the tide, for a sailing vessel must arrive off Lydney pier if possible at slack tide, otherwise she may be swept so far above the pier that, by the time she is able to return on the ebb, the tide is too strong to attempt an entrance even if the gates were open. At spring tides about 15 minutes before high water the tide starts to ease, and by the same amount of time – or less – after high water the ebb is running at its maximum speed.

Now although that morning (my first sight ever of Lydney pier) we headed the *Jane* downstream, and had a nice steady easterly wind for so doing, we were still travelling stern first towards the pier, the tide being stronger than the wind. Capt Smart kept watching the time and calculating the distance yet to travel, judging our speed astern by the changing position of the landmarks ashore, talking meanwhile of sundry subjects with no sign of anxiety – master of a situation he had been in many times before. In later years, seeing men – even in vessels with auxiliary engines – pale

and anxious in similar situations off Lydney pier, I would think of
Capt Smart and marvel at his ability. We were getting nearer the
pier now; soon we saw vessels leaving the locks, but being swept
up by the tide immediately they left the shelter of the pier. But the
tide was easing. 'We'll jibe her over now,' said the Captain. Then,
'Haul the sheets in, we'll get on up.' So on the starboard tack we
edged towards the Lydney shore still being swept up river with the
last of the flood. Soon came the call 'Take the topsail down', then,
'Haul down the flying jib', followed by 'Lower the anchor down
to the forefoot, quickly now!' By the time I had executed those
orders I saw we were quite near the pier, and the skipper was
keeping the *Jane*'s head downstream for the last few minutes of the
flood. Then a raucous shout from the pier-head, 'Come on ahead
Jane, there's no tide here now.' Meantime I had by now got a
heavy manila warp ready on the starboard quarter with a bowline
ready to drop over a bollard to act as a stern rope to bring the
vessel up.

My orders then were as soon as the vessels bow was in past the
pierhead to haul down the two jibs, and then haul up the tack of
the mainsail and mizzen, but to leave the handling of the stern
warp to the captain. This meant, of course, and rightly so, that he
was afraid to trust me to take the way off the vessel and bring her
up by quickly putting the warp in the chock and lead it to the cavil
and put the proper turns thereon, surge the rope enough not to
part it, yet as little as possible so as to bring the vessel to a standstill
in the shortest possible length. To fumble that particular exercise
could easily result in a man losing a leg or a hand if caught in a
coil. Also should the rope jam on the cavil, it would at best part
the rope, but it might pull the cavil from the stanchions or take
some of the bulwarks as well, leaving the vessel to forge ahead and
maybe damage herself or some other craft. But all was well on that
great day at Lydney. I hauled down 'my jibs', hauled up the tacks
of main and mizzen. Capt Smart brought the *Jane* up by the stern
warp in just over her own length. We had sailed into the lock
without fuss, and without comment from anybody on the performance. It was not unusual; men did it everyday, as my father had
done 40 years before. With regard to my mention above, of my
having to lower the anchor down to the forefoot of the vessel, this
was a precautionary measure in case the bow of the ship should
strike on the quay wall or some other vessel and so drive the anchor
through her bow.

With regard to my foregoing remarks concerning Capt Smart's
ability and seamanship, this, of course, I only realised as time

passed and I had experienced the difficulty other men had in carrying out the same operations. In later years I was truly thankful that such a man had been my first instructor in things to do with the sea and ships. I must add here too that Capt Smart was not, strictly speaking, a trowman. He had served in deep-water sailing ships and had plenty of coastwise experience. At one time he owned a little vessel, the *Martin Luther*; it was only in later life he became part owner in the *Jane*. But he knew the Severn, and the trows were rigged much the same as scores of other vessels that were designed and built to voyage farther afield in more turbulent seas. Good trowmen were good Severn men and Capt Smart certainly knew the Severn. Another mark of distinction with regard to Capt Smart was that in the *Jane* we had a teapot – and used it – instead of just the kettle.

That same afternoon we went under one of the coal tips on the canal and loaded the *Jane's* eight 10-ton trucks with Forest of Dean coal. We, the crew, did not touch the cargo; coal trimmers shovelled the coal into the farthest corners of the hold and filled her level through to give her the right trim. By the time we had put the hatches on and then the hatch-cloths and battened down, washed down and scrubbed the decks, until not a bit of coal dust could be seen, and hauled the vessel to a berth across the canal, it was past 5 pm. Therefore since 4.30 am on the previous day when we hove the anchor and left the River Axe we had been 'on the go' for over 36 hours, except for the four hours' sleep we managed to get off Clevedon. Utterly weary, and again too tired to eat my tea, I fell asleep on the hard forecastle locker; romance had been replaced by reality.

We sailed from Lydney on the next morning tide much refreshed after a long night in the bunk. The wind must have been about south east, for I recall we sailed most of the way to Portishead on the port tack. We could not have made the River Axe on that ebb, so we anchored in Portishead to await the next ebb. By this time the cabin floor needed a scrub out, likewise the forecastle. Of course, the captain would not stoop to such menial work, so that left only me! That night at high water we again set the mainsail and mizzen and hove up our anchor and proceeded on our way, and the wind again being favourable we reached the mouth of the Axe and anchored in what was then known as the hole (in later years the hole silted up).

Now there was still about a mile of the river to navigate to reach the coal wharf at Uphill. With a breeze from the west or west by south it was quite possible to sail up as far as what we called the

Pill with just the mizzen and a jib. Here a vessel had to be checked around the point with a warp ashore, out of the main stream into the slacker water of the Pill. Even here with the same wind a jib would give her enough way to take her right into her berth. But more often it meant warping her into the berth.

Should the wind be directly blowing out of the river so that no sail could be used to get the *Jane* (or any other vessel in any other river) from the river's mouth to the discharging wharf, a simple alternative was available. This was to 'drop' the vessel up stern first with the tidal stream, using her anchor as a drogue – we termed this drudging. But it was strenuous work if only two men were aboard. When the state of the tide provided sufficient water to start the exercise the cable would be hove short with the stock of the anchor – in theory, as it could not be seen – just clear of the bottom, thus allowing the anchor to waggle from side to side and the fluke to plough, as it were, through the mud or sand as the vessel started to drag the anchor at the moment she proceeded stern first with the tide.

The captain would now be at the helm, so that should the bow of the vessel sheer off towards either bank, the movement of the rudder would bring her head back to mid-stream. Should the ship be dropping astern too fast – or going as fast, or nearly as fast, as the stream the rudder would be useless, as the current would not give it any purchase. The captain would then shout, 'Give her some chain – quickly now' (it was always 'quickly now' in the *Jane*!); this extra cable would allow the anchor to 'dig in' and slow her movement astern; she would now respond to her rudder and could be 'steered' sternwards as before. Then again should the water become more shallow, causing the anchor to 'dig in' too much, thus slowing the sternway of the ship, some chain would have to be hove in by the man forward. This was where a third hand was needed (if the economies prevailing allowed) otherwise the captain would have to dash forward and supply the necessary manpower to break the anchor out. Back again at the wheel he would soon again be calling our 'give her a bit more chain' or 'heave in a few feet if you can, quickly now!'

This exercise could be carried out in most rivers on both the ebb and flood tide and, if the vessel was *loaded*, against even a fairly strong wind. In a light vessel it would need to be calm otherwise the ship would be wind-rode. The alternative then would be to warp her up (or down) the river. This meant taking a kedge anchor ahead with the ship's boat. The kedge would be placed in the stern of the boat with the stock inboard and a fluke hanging over the transom. A light coir 3-inch line would be attached to the kedge and 60 or 80 fathom of line carefully coiled on the stern sheets. The other end of the line would be attached to the top barrel of the dolly winch aboard the vessel. The man in the boat would then scull away by using a very flexible ash oar in the sculling notch in the transom. When the last of the line had run out, the boatman would grasp the kedge by the stock and heave it over the side taking care to keep the flukes in a position so that one would dig in immediately it hit the bottom.

But with only a two-man crew this was not so very satisfactory, as it meant the man aboard had on occasion to run aft to shift the helm and dash forward again to heave it on the winch. With a three-man crew it was a very practical method. In the early 1920s, the writer can recall being the boatman when a vessel was kedged from Bideford to Appledore, a distance of about two and a half miles against a head wind, but there were two good men on the winch and a skipper at the helm. The vessel was light and the crew were exhausted – except the skipper!

Readers may wonder after reading the above why a tug was not hired to tow a vessel in such circumstances, rather than all the work and time entailed with anchors, warps and kedges. The answer is that in isolated rivers such as the Axe or the Yeo no tugs were available; even if there had been it is doubtful if one could have been afforded with the poor freights then prevailing. In any case from the mouth of the river a vessel could dredge up on one flood tide, therefore as she could only be got into her berth at high water the services of a tug could not have seen her tied up any sooner.

The quarry at Uphill was only about 150 yards away from the Pill where the *Jane* had her berth, and the walling stones were hauled from the quarry to the vessel by horse and tip-cart (we called it a 'putt') then tipped down a steel-lined wooden shoot into the hold.

Sometimes when there was not sufficient stone ready for a full cargo some more stone had to be got out by drilling holes and placing a powder charge therein and blasting the stone from the face of the quarry. On quite a few occasions I was asked by the foreman to come and turn the drill. The drill was a steel shaft about ¾″ diameter about 5 feet long with diamond-shaped cutting edges flared out so that they were slightly wider than the shank of the drill. With me to hold the drill, three men instead of the usual two were able to each have a sledge hammer to drive the drill into the rock whilst I held the drill upright and with each blow of a hammer I had to twist the drill around about a third of its circumference, thus the cutting edges would with every twist, cut (or break?) away, and reduce to dust, the base of the hole and slowly deepen it. A short drill was necessary at first to enable the hammermen to be able to strike it 'good and hard'. When it became too low to strike without bending low a longer drill replaced the first. At first I was in fear that one might miss the drill and strike my hands, but this never happened.

When the hole was six or eight feet deep black powder was poured in from a flask (or measure) then the necessary fuse cable was inserted and the hole filled to the top with stone dust rammed hard. We would then all crouch behind a bank of earth and the foreman would press the plunger. The charge would lift out anything from 10 to 30 tons of stone, or it might just 'blow out' the drill hole. For myself the blowing was great fun; the ground where we crouched 50 yards away would seem to lift and sway coupled with the exciting roar and smoke of the blast.

I suppose that one of the greatest hazards, if not *the* greatest, of the River Severn at the time when I was a lad, was sailing a vessel through the Shoots with a baffling wind. Bound from Kingroad to Lydney with a light ship it was usual to leave early on the flood tide so as to get through the Shoots before the English Stones were covered, thus, especially with a light wind, forestalling the danger of the vessel getting swept over the rocks to the eastward. Between our old enemy the Gruggy Rock and the edge of the English Stones the distance is about 1½ cables wide (300 yards) and this is the narrowest part. In my opinion the worst wind a vessel could have on entering the pull of the Shoots was a light fair wind. With the tide running through at four or five knots, a vessel would lose what wind was in her sails and become as a ship becalmed, at the mercy of the fierce eddies and whirlpools usually experienced in that very narrow neck of water. Far better to have a light head wind which the speed of the current would transform into a commanding breeze, so that the ship responded easily and quickly to her helm.

On quite a few occasions after leaving Lydney in the *Jane* (a deck trow with a cargo capacity of 80 tons) bound for the river Axe with only Capt Smart and myself on board, the favourable wind he had at first either became very light or completely died away. If this happened after we passed the Lyde Rock – and if the wind was northerly the stronger tide easily accounted for this – it usually meant I had to get the boat ready to go ahead of the vessel to act as a tiny tug boat. To do this we in the *Jane* usually hauled down the outer jib, which was not much use anyway with no wind, and used the down-haul as a tow rope, this rope being attached to the jib at the extreme end of the bowsprit and the hauling part made fast in the boat; one had a towrope of some 60 feet long plus the length of the bowsprit – about 22 feet, so that the boat was about 80 feet ahead of the ship. The end of this 'towrope', as it now was, was always made fast to the after thwart with a 'slipperly hitch', which was just one turn around the thwart and one half hitch with the looped end showing and only needed a sharp tug to untie itself. 'Don't forget now!' the skipper would bawl. 'A slippery hitch with plenty of end showing.'

Now a teenage boy in a ship's boat, in the fierce tides of the Severn, sculling up under a ship's bow and taking the 'towrope' may seem, to a layman, an extremely dangerous operation, but this was not so, for the vessel having very little, or no way of her own, the ship and the boat were both being swept down together at the same speed. But the danger lay in the whirlpools in the Shoots. I must point out here that the boat was not so much used to tow the vessel, but to cant her. Should she be heading too much to one side of the fairway the captain would shout to the man in the boat to pull off whichever bow was necessary to get her back to midstream.

Thus the heavy trow's boat being pulled vigorously at right angles to the ship's head, and the light towrope made fast to the very end of her long bowsprit exerted quite an amount of purchase, and usually the vessel's heading would be seen to alter almost immediately. To assist in this manoeuvre the captain on board would have a large sweep (a large oar perhaps 20 feet long with a 6-foot blade) shipped over the rail in a loop of rope made fast to the main rigging. He might have to stand on the main hatchway to get the correct balance then, after dipping the huge blade in the water, he could either walk forward and push, or walk back and pull to help the man in the boat alter the heading of the ship. Immediately she started to cant the call would come, 'Straight ahead now, quickly now!' When the vessel was canted athwart the current, especially in the swiftly running Shoots, she would catch a breeze at the same speed as the stream and thus forge ahead with enough way to be put about on the other tack.

When this happened the man in the boat would slip the towrope which could easily be picked up again from under the bowsprit. With regard to the whirlpools that were always apparent in the Shoots during high spring tides, these would suddenly appear caused by the swift currents and eddies diverted by obstructions below. Sometimes two would appear together and, should the boat be off at right angles to the vessel whilst trying to cant her and be caught in a 'swirl', as we called it, the boat could not be handled by the oars for she would be 'jaw locked' as it were and in danger, with the towline taut as it would be, of being swung in an arc and crashing back into the side of the ship. This is where the 'slippery hitch' came in – a sharp tug at the loose end of the line set the boat free and she could again be handled and pulled back under the bowsprit where the towrope could be grasped and quickly made fast again.

This exercise has taken some time to write about, but actually only minutes were involved in jumping into the boat, attaching the 'towrope' and pulling away ahead of the ship. The distance through the Shoots from the Charston Rock is under two miles, therefore if we say the speed of the current was five or six knots, half an hour would see the ship clear.

If when coming past the Lyde Rock with a cargo from Lydney with the wind westerly and there was a heavy sea over the benches (an outfall below the Lyde) and the weather too menacing, we would go into the mouth of the river Wye until it fined down. We could not be 'hard weather men' in the elderly *Jane*.

During these journeys to Lydney I saw many sailing vessels of all types. Capt Smart kept the little *Jane* very smart, clean and shipshape and I thought she was wonderful. But I was overawed at the sight of the many beautiful vessels so graceful and tall, with bows that flared outwards and swept upwards, thrusting towards the sky beautifully kept bowsprits, some with jib-booms seeming to rear right up as high as our *Jane*'s mizzen. Then the lovely figureheads picked out in gold and brilliant white paint by some careful hand. The general appearance from stem to stern was more than just smartness – a revelation of the feeling of pride that prevailed throughout the ship. These, of course, were coasting vessels: big able ketches like the lovely *Sunshine* and the *Irene*; schooners such as the *Welcome*, the *Welcome Home*, and the *Earl Cairns*, the latter vessel now, 60 years later, a desolate hulk stripped of her planking lying in Deadman's Creek on the Penryn River. These lovely ships fired me with a new ambition, an overwhelming desire to sail in one. But there were other trows there as well, trows nearly twice the size of the *Jane* and quite good and able vessels, well kept with huge long bowsprits, but the difference was there – beside the smart and lofty coasters they looked box-like and somewhat ugly. Poor lowly, but indispensable little vessels.

Came the time when the *Jane* had to go into Gardiner's Yard at Lydney for repairs to her bulwarks and decks. The yard which was adjacent, and north east of the pier, also had a gridiron. The owner of the yard at that time 1919-1920 (or he may have been the tenant) was Mr Alec Gardiner. Mr Gardiner was a shipwright but, like most men of his kind in those days, he also did his own black-smithing. Capt Smart lent me to Mr Gardiner to help in the black-smith's shop – thereby saving some labour costs for the work that had to be done. When any ironwork had to be made up, I acted as 'striker' on the anvil. The blacksmith would heat up the wrought iron – I was also the bellow's boy – and when it was white hot the smith would whip it out of the fire with the tongs in his left hand, place it on the anvil and start to fashion it with a two-pound hammer, whilst I used a seven-pound hammer with a long shaft. Every time the smith struck a blow with his two-pounder, I im-mediately followed with a blow in the same place with my seven-pound hammer, whilst the smith turned and twisted the piece of iron to draw it out or flatten it as he wanted. He had to work fast, and I with the heavier tool had to keep time, blow for blow. The face of the hammers had to strike the hot iron flat, otherwise the edge of the hammers would dent the work. Should the shaft of my hammer not be level when the tool struck, the blacksmith would shout, 'Lower your hand and strike light!' This meant I had struck too hard without bending my back! Every time the piece of iron we were fashioning was withdrawn from the fire and we started beating it into shape with the hammers, the white hot sparks, turning red as they danced away from the anvil, streaked away like tiny meteors into the gloom at the rear of the forge. Nearly 60 years later these beautiful fleeting pictures remain on call in my mind.

Immediately the object was finished it was plunged into Stock-holm tar (maybe with something else with it) so that the tar was actually burnt into the iron. This was termed 'Swedish galvanising'. Although my arms ached after the first day on the hammer, I was hefty and strong and soon got used to the speed of the swift striking with the seven-pounder. When I went aboard the *Jane* for my meals, Capt Smart would tell me he had heard Mr Gardiner calling out over the din of hammers, 'Lower your hand – and strike light!' (Not strike lightly!!)

During this same time at Gardiner's Yard, the little trow *Industry* came to the yard to go on the gridiron for some repairs to her bottom. Her planking below the waterline was very dirty, so it had to be scrubbed off and scraped. Mr Gardiner offered me sixpence an hour if I would do the job for him. He said he had Capt Smart's permission to ask me. I recall how amazed I was at the high rate of pay offered, for my father at that time was paying his labourers,

and they were married men, eighteen shillings for a 44-hour week
(less than two new pence per hour). The gridiron as it was called
(we in the vessels always called it 'the block') was merely long
baulks of timber about one foot square bolted and dogged together,
laid on top of each other four high and fixed athwartships. There
were about 12 rows of these spaced to accommodate vessels up to
and perhaps over 100 feet long. The gridiron was situated on the
bank of the river and low enough so that a vessel could be floated
on or off at average spring tides. This meant that the timber staging
(or floor) that was provided for the shipwrights to work from and
which was level with the base of the timber baulks, was covered
by most of the tides at highwater and, the Severn being an extremely
muddy river, a lot of sediment was left on the staging in the form
of slurry. This had to be scrubbed away as the tide receded otherwise it was almost impossible to work. I had to do this every day
before I could start my scraping. It was a race against time, otherwise the fast falling tide in the Severn would ebb clear of the staging
before I could clean away the slurry. One certainly earned the 'rate
for the job'.

The scrapers used for scraping the old pitch – from the seams –
and blistered tar from the bottom were mostly made from large
and wide old files and rasps. These were heated in the forge, beaten
out and turned over at the end then tempered so that they could
always be sharpened with a file. Mr Gardiner gave me a pair of
goggles to use to keep the pitch dust out of my eyes. One had to
kneel down when working close to the keel, or crouch as there was
only four feet of headroom in the centre of the ship, It was very
hot work, for the scraper was heavy and one had to look upwards.
I found the goggles kept getting misted-up, so after a few hours I
took them off to be better able to see. But the pitch was hard and
brittle and would hop and fly away from the scraper. Before long
my eyes started to smart and, although I put the goggles on again,
they got worse; even my back and chest were irritating from the
dust. By the end of the day I was unable to open my eyes and got
into trouble for not using the goggles – no wonder the rate of pay
was high. I was given some lotion and advised to bathe my eyes
every hour and this, aided with some salty language from Capt
Smart, enabled me, after a couple of days, to restart the work.

I believe my pay per trip for a cargo of stone from Uphill to the
Kingston Seymour Walls was ten shillings, including, of course,
loading and discharging the vessel. If we sailed from the Kingston
Walls to load a cargo of coal from Lydney for the River Axe, I got
another 25 shillings, making 35 shillings in all for the two cargoes.

But for a straight trip to Lydney from Uphill and back with a cargo of coal was 30/-. This was when there was only Capt Smart and myself aboard. The ship provided the food. I recall that this was filling but not too lavish. My pay whilst in Gardiner's dockyard at Lydney was ten shillings per week, but whilst I was working on the *Industry* for my sixpence an hour, I got no pay from the ship, but my helping in the blacksmith's shop paid for my 'board and lodging' in the *Jane*. We were three weeks at Lydney and for me it was a glorious golden harvest. I had never had so much money! No question then of breaking some silly rules for working too many hours a day; no fear of some watchful and disapproving eye of someone eager to report the dreadful sin of a sailor boy swinging a hammer in a smithy's shop, infringing the rules of some union, the rules of which now bind men with bonds like steel.

It was during this particular time at Lydney that I first saw the lovely little ketch the *Isabella*. She was lying beside the bank in the canal loaded with coal and ready to sail for Youghal in southern Ireland. With her white decks and lovely spars she looked, to me, like a beautiful yacht. I could not keep my eyes off her. One day her captain came back, I heard his name was Jones. He was a small slight man and was wearing a smart suit. Len Gardiner, the lockgate man – son of Mr Gardiner the shipwright – said he looked like a bank manager (but I had never seen a bank manager). My disappointment (at his appearance) was short-lived, for when the *Isabella* left Lydney the next day Capt Jones looked, and sounded, what he was: a competent master at home in his ship. We were still in Gardiner's yard with the *Jane* when the news was brought back from Ireland that Capt Jones's son, who had been one of the crew of the *Isabella*, had been shot whilst ashore in Youghal and killed by the IRA. That was nearly 60 years ago, yet today the same conflict with its hate and cruel affliction prevails.

When that sad news was related to us Capt Smart, knowing how I hankered to be in the vessels trading to Ireland, gave me a meaning look and said: 'That is what comes of being in the Irish trade.'

My father who had sailed in the trows during the last quarter of the 19th century could recall seeing as many as 60 sail, mostly trows, in Lydney canal and basin at one time. And in Bridgwater Bay in favourable weather often ten or a dozen sail jockeying about, waiting for sufficient water into the River Parrett. Although I have never heard any actual figures, according to the many accounts I heard in my early life, many vessels with their crews were lost on the dreaded tail of the Gore Sands. From Bleadon Hill one can see even in a moderate gale of wind, the seething white water, leaping high, as the seas break on the tail of the Gore, the spume turning to smoke as it is caught up by the wind and swept away. One can imagine the last moments of the crew of a trow caught in its shrieking fury as the vessel struck the treacherous sands.

During the years following the First World War, the time of which I write the trade from Lydney had diminished to a mere fraction of what it was pre-war. The reasons were many and have been put on record by various people who suffered during the aftermath of the war.

The *Jane*, her repairs completed, loaded a cargo of house coal for the merchant at Uphill. There were two Bideford vessels in the basin with us the morning we were leaving Lydney, and the Sharpness tug came over to Lydney pier to take them in tow. The wind was from the west, and Capt Smart told me the two 'Barmen' as he called them, were employing the tug because, being loaded, they would not risk beating down the Severn so they each paid £1 for the tow to Kingroad, which of course served as a pilot as well. But the *Jane* did not take a tug, for £1 at that time was a week's wages for the majority of manual workers. Had we taken a tug no time would have been saved for we should have anchored at Portishead in any case. It was not possible to reach the River Axe on one ebb from Lydney. When it is high water at Lydney there is an hour's ebb in the Axe River. We did not need the topsail on that trip down the Severn, it was tacking all the way until we got to Charston Rock. There we found plenty of wind for the elderly *Jane* but our course then bringing the wind abeam, we hoisted the main tack and the old vessel seemed to gallop through the shoots as if anxious to get home. We reached the Axe on the next ebb, then after four or five hours' sleep, the wind being offshore, we were preparing to drudge up to the coal berth. They were waiting for the coal; we had been away a long time. At the entrance to the Pill that led from the main stream to the berth, the quarrymen were waiting to take a line to tow us to the quay; this was about a quarter of a mile. During this 'tow' I had to get the hatch cloths off and the hatches stacked away ready for discharging, for the horses and carts were waiting to be loaded. Safely in her berth before highwater we got the loading gaff up and rigged with the ginny wheel and whip, and then, after a few minutes to make and drink a cup of tea, the work of discharging started. My job was on the dolly winch.

Looking back as I write to nearly 60 years ago, one marvels at the amount of work and the number of hours a man had to put in for the few shillings' reward he received. It was hard work in all weathers: anchor drill, for all the trows carried plenty of 'ground gear' as it was called; sail drill; boat ahead in a calm and at the end of the journey the crew were expected to set the pace when discharging, or loading, as the case may be. There were no drones in those vessels, there were no hiding places for them; one drone would have been half the crew, or nearly so; it would have been an impossible situation. Of course there were bad men and dishonest men as in every other walk of life, but they were willing and lively and attached to their vessels, and there was plenty of excitement and variety.

During the years before the First World War when I was a small boy, the Weston Clevedon and Portishead Light Railway had built a concrete pier on the west bank of the River Yeo, adjacent to the bridge that carried the railway over that river. A rail track was laid to connect the pier to the main line so that railway waggons could be shunted right beside the proposed discharging berth. The purpose of this terminal, the local people understood, was to establish and develop sea-borne trade in addition to the transport of coal for their own locomotives. Then came the 1914 war and the pier was never used until the early 1920s.

It was probably about the year 1919 when my father was approached by the Light Railway Company, and undertook the work of clearing the bottom of the River Yeo of all stakes, posts and piles and any other projections that might be a hazard to a ship's bottom or propellers – all except rock, but there was no rock in the Yeo. The 'obstructions' were mainly fencing and gate posts which many, many years before must have been erected on the saltings as fences to farm boundaries, also as groins across gullies on the saltings. But all had over countless years gradually slid down to the river's bottom owing to erosion caused by the torrents of flood water the river carried away from the inland levels it served. I assisted in the work. It was quite simple. A boat was launched from the railway's pier when no tidal water was in the river; there was usually plenty of fresh water running to sea from the drainage rhines inland, quite sufficient to float a boat. But the 'crew' had to be lively, for in some places the river's bottom was wide and shallow, in others the channel was deep and narrow forming rapids that raced along in the most exciting fashion. The posts and stakes were sawn off as low as possible; mostly they were iron hard and only the hearts were left, the knots protruding from the hearts like mighty pegs. None of the stakes or posts would float, everything had to be taken ashore in the boat. It was a change from the sea walls.

Then came the news that a motor vessel was expected with a
cargo of steam coal for the railway locomotives. This sensational
news was followed by a request to my father from the Light
Railway management to 'keep a look out' for the ship and supply
any assistance necessary. We were not told what kind of help.
Some time later we saw a vessel off St Thomas's Head heading in
on the early flood around the point. In the slack water inside the
point we saw her topsail come down, then the headsails – she had
anchored. We did not for a minute think this could be the 'motor
vessel' bound for the Yeo. Soon we saw a boat put off from the
vessel and pull in to the rocky shore of Woodspring Hill. On that
quiet and lonely shore it was like a scene from a smuggler's story.
Later, we could see two men like two ants climbing up in the green
sward of the hill and my father thought they were gaining elevation
to enable them to locate the mouth of the Yeo. The mouth of that
river ran out through the mud flats, fanning out and blending so
well with the surroundings that it could not be seen from seaward.
There were four of us working on that part of the walls near the
river and, at my father's suggestion we all shouted together the
word 'ahoy!' Our distance from Woodspring was about one and
a quarter miles or more but we saw the two specks stop and turn
about. They had certainly heard us. One of the masons hoisted an
old coat on a long batten and waved it furiously in the air, and
immediately the specks came quickly down over the sward. Soon
we saw the boat put off to the vessel; the jibs were set and it was
not long before the vessel was abreast of the river's mouth and,
being now half flood, not far from the base of the walls. By that
time I had recognised the vessel as the flush-deck trow *Sarah*; I
had seen her at Lydney when she was not a motor vessel. After
dropping her anchor again the crew came in to the walls with their
boat. They were the same two men I had met at Lydney and they
were Appledore men, two cousins, and their name was Screech.
Here were two young and experienced coastwise seamen glad to
have a job in a trow in the upper Bristol Channel, and I recalled
the remarks made at Lydney that 'it showed the state of affairs in
Appledore when two such men had work short handed in a trow'.
To return to the cargo for the Yeo, Capt Screech told us he had
no chart aboard that showed the Yeo River. But he said, 'Us knew
'twas somewhere back of St Thomas's Head!' and looking back at
Woodspring Hill in wonder, both men agreed they had never heard
fellows 'holler so loud before'. But when the wind and sea were
quiet that was a silent and peaceful shore, and the mud flats when
uncovered by the sea magnified and carried any sound like some

mighty sounding board. We then heard that the *Sarah* was the 'motor vessel' expected! A 15 h.p. Kelvin engine had been installed in Appledore with the propeller shaft through her quarter. We learned they had very little engine fuel aboard. 'Hope 'tis enough to get us up the river,' they said. We guessed the reason for this. It also explained the reason for no chart – no funds. Probably the usual advance on the freight from the broker at Newport, where the vessel loaded, had been sent home to their wives, such was the state of affairs. Men were working vessels for extremely meagre rewards. My father and I went off with the crew in the boat to the *Sarah*. Captain Screech, never having been to the river before, was glad to meet someone with local knowledge. It was about a mile from the river's mouth to the Railway's pier. Except for the few trows that had, at odd times, taken shelter in the mouth of the Yeo when it proved to be imprudent to berth on the open shore at the foot of the sea walls to discharge their cargoes of stone the *Sarah*, as far as we knew, was the first vessel ever to bring a cargo to be discharged actually in our river. The *Sarah* could carry 120 tons and had a draught of about eight and a half feet. To me she looked water-washed and shabby, and exceedingly tidy and shipshape around her decks and in her rigging. But the oakum had spewed out of the seams of the planking of her hull indicating that her hull had been working under stress in not the best of weather. This was confirmed when Capt Screech told us that they had recently made two trips to Ireland and back to the English Channel!

There are no hazards in the Yeo, only mud, but it was a good job we had cleared the bottom of the stakes and other obstructions with the vessel's propeller shaft through her quarter! The Kelvin was started. I was more than thrilled; it was the first engine I had ever seen in a vessel, my father likewise. After the first noisy splutter it settled down to a rhythmical beat; even on the fore deck one could feel the gentle throb as if the little vessel really had a heart. However, no sails were furled before we got to the pier. The little engine could only push the bluff bowed *Sarah* through the water at about three miles per hour but, with a little tide to help us, we arrived at the pier in less than half an hour. No sail handling – one just stood around whilst the Kelvin plutted away. To me it seemed unnatural and some how wrong.

We quickly tied up at the pier and by now the full tide in the river had lifted the vessel high enough for us to see the surrounding countryside over the banks of the river. Kingston Seymour is approximately nine feet below sea level at mean high water, the eye-level of the crew of the *Sarah*, therefore, was about 18 feet above the surface of the countryside near the coast and for many miles in all directions inland. In addition to this there were no dwellings of any description anywhere near the pier; the nearest shop was about one and a half miles, and the nearest inn – the 'Full Quart' of Hewish – two miles walk away and across many fields and ditches! This seemed most surprising, and very disappointing to the two mariners, for they were short of stores, and now being late evening had no hope of getting any.

The Railway Co. had installed a steam crane to lift the coal out of the vessels, but even for those days it was old-fashioned with an upright boiler and a tall stove-pipe chimney. The bucket held about 10 cwt, and, wheezing and rattling, the old crane would wind up the bucket and swing it in over the railway waggon where the tipper would be waiting to knock out the catch which held the tub upright, thus allowing it to capsize into the truck. That was the theory of the exercise, but only too often as the jib swung round bringing the bucket swinging and spinning over the waggon it did not stop but came to a halt past its objective. The only method the tipper could adopt was to judge the instant to make a leap and knock out the catch as the bucket swung and spun over the waggon, but only by great agility could he expect to survive. I can vouch for this for I was the first tipper ever to pit my wits and speed against the monster. The fault may have been the driver, he was one of the locomotive drivers, but he blamed the brakes. I took that job on to oblige Capt Screech, there not being a third hand in the vessel (the two crew shovelled all the coal out of the hold). After the first couple of buckets one was as black as the coal and for this I was paid ¾d per ton, or seven shillings and sixpence for the 120 tons. This nearly 60 years later may seem ludicrous, but by the current standards it was good pay; the work was completed in one and a half days. My father's men on the sea walls were paid three shillings per day.

The freight per ton for a cargo of coal from Newport (where the *Sarah* loaded) was about two shillings and threepence per ton and the crew were working her by the 'thirds'. The whole freight for a full cargo of 120 tons would amount to £13, the share for the crew would be four pounds ten shillings, the same amount for the ship's expenses, and the other share for the owners. As the Screech's were working the vessel two-handed, it was most likely shared two pounds ten shillings for the master and two pounds for the mate, but they would have to share the cost of the tipper mentioned above. With three hands their share of the freight may have been divided thus: two pounds for the master, 30 shillings for the mate and a pound for the third hand. Each would pay their share of the food. If the trade was there it would have been possible for the *Sarah*, from the near South Wales ports, to manage two cargoes a week, weather permitting, or in any case three cargoes in a fortnight. The latter would have earned the master three pounds per week. My father at that time would have been paying his stone masons sevenpence per hour, or about 27 shillings per week. So even at one cargo per week the *Sarah*'s crew would be much better paid than workers ashore.

The trade to the River Yeo never developed to any great extent. It was mainly steam coal for the railway's own locomotives. The Light Railway was really managed from offices in London and their knowledge of sea borne trade appeared to be limited. The Light Railway only served three towns: Weston-super-Mare, Clevedon and Portishead, and as coal could be taken to each of these places by small vessels, it would not have been economical to off-load on to the Railway at Yeo pier and handle the cargo again at one of the three terminals. Hence the lack of trade.

Trading to Ireland in the ketch Garlandstone

It was after one of the *Sarah*'s subsequent visits to the Yeo, and the day after she left there for Lydney, that a telegram arrived asking me if I could join the ketch *Garlandstone* as mate. The captain of the *Sarah* had, it appears, recommended me. The wages were £8.00 per month, and as the job also included my board, this was more than double the masons earned (or got) on the walls. My father tried to dissuade me, with so many vessels tied up he said 'there must be something wrong, why send for you?'

I found the *Garlandstone* lying loaded in the Lydney canal. Having never seen her before I was happy to find such a pretty little vessel, with a beautifully rounded counter stern: a sharp and jaunty bow, even her sides showed a gentle curve throughout, and the narrow planking of her deck followed that beautiful curve. She had a wheelhouse with a half curved back; a roomy galley and most welcome of all (to me at least), a curved back toilet like a sentry box forward of the fore rigging. This latter luxury would be unusual in a trow. She looked new and at that time was about 14 years old. A big and tall man on her deck wearing a stiff collar and a bowler hat introduced himself to me. He was Andrew Murdock, her master and owner. Capt Murdock wore a bowler hat at sea and ashore; the only other kind of headgear I ever saw him wear was a southwester. He explained the bowler when saying he was always knocking his head against the deck beams in the forecastle and the bowler was protection.

The crews' quarters were in the forecastle because the *Garlandstone* had an engine installed in the after cabin. But the forecastle had been enlarged by pushing back the bulkhead. There was a small room for the privacy of the master on the starboard side and one for the mate on the port side. Right forward were two bunks for the other hands, but only one was ever needed. A nice table and seatlockers were convenient to all, and a closed ornamental fireplace with a mantelpiece over made a very comfortable setup.

The cabin aft was taken up by the engine. I cannot recall either the horse power or the make of that engine. But I know it had a French name that began with the letters 'D.J.' Capt Murdock told me it was French. He also told me that the engine was very costly to run and that he only used it in the Severn, or in rivers and entering and leaving harbours. I found this to be true – even when we had hardly any wind to sail, but it suited me, for I never took to engines. The *Garlandstone* was bound to Countmacsherry in Southern Ireland with a cargo of 120 tons of house coal.

We left Lydney the next morning. I remember the surprise I felt when Capt Murdock told me to get the boat alongside to be hauled aboard. This was a thing Capt Smart, when we saw any sailing vessel with an auxiliary engine get her boat aboard before leaving Lydney or Sharpness, always condemned. He thought it a most foolhardy thing to do, for should the engine fail at a critical moment and there was no wind, the boat, towing astern, might be the crew's only hope. 'No Severn man would ever do it,' he used to say. Now Capt Murdock was a Gloucester man, hence my surprise. It must be borne in mind that at the time of which I write engines to us were something new and therefore suspect.

No heaving the vessel ahead in the basin with the aid of the dolly winch on that morning of departure. With the engine ticking over causing the little ship to tremble throughout her length, we waited for the order to 'come ahead'. When it came we hauled in the mooring ropes and Capt Murdock, himself at the wheel, put the engine ahead with a control lever beside him; the trembling was replaced by a shudder as the *Garlandstone* forged ahead, and within two minutes was out into the Severn heading over the Saniger Sands towards the opposite shore. This departure to me was a new and exciting experience. Here was quite a change in performance. No pushing the vessel off with the boathook if the wind was 'on the pier' until 'one's eyes struck fire' as we called it. Or dragging an 8-inch towrope about the decks if the vessel took a tug; there was nothing to do!

Capt Murdock stood at the wheel, a tall imposing figure wearing his bowler hat and shore-going clothes, looking quite unlike a nautical man. Many Gloucester men seemed to adopt his manner of dress (except the bowler). It was as if they felt that the less nautical they looked the better whereas the Appledore men, and

this includes most of the sailors from over 'the bar', could always
be identified for what they were.

There was a third hand in the *Garlandstone*. He had joined her
about a week before I did. His name was Jack; if I ever heard his
surname I have forgotten it. Jack was a little bird-like Cockney
man and appeared to be a bit of a tramp, but a likeable tramp. One
trip in the *Garlandstone* was more than enough for him. But he
was quite a passable cook. That morning whilst we motored down
the Severn he made us a splendid breakfast. This was to me quite
a social advancement: cooked in the galley and taken to our quarters
forward on a tray which had high sides like bulwarks. Then again
there was a teapot, all of which gladdened my heart. Of course,
the captain went down to breakfast first whilst I took the wheel.
The little vessel steered like a fish; motoring as she was, she would
respond to half a spoke of the wheel. The fact that I had been
recommended for the berth I had in such a vessel brought me a
feeling of pleasure and pride which I did my best to conceal.

We anchored off Portishead, for there was a nasty head wind
and soon it would be low water. Not far away from us was the
two-masted schooner *Via*. The master and owner of her was also
a Gloucester man, Capt Harper; by a coincidence she was also
bound for Courtmacsherry. Here at anchor I had time to accustom
myself to the different set-up of the rigging and running gear which,
though generally the same, is always subject to the sundry whims
and ideas of different masters.

The *Garlandstone*'s topsail did not tie up aloft, but was sent up
'flying' on a wire jack-stay which was rove through the hanks on
the luff of the sail as it was hauled up by the halyards. When the
sail was aloft the jackstay was then bowsed down to an eye-bolt in
the deck near the foot of the mast, thus keeping the luff of the sail
tight to the topmast, the tack of the sail being hauled down taut by
a small tackle. The sheet of the topsail was permanently rove off
through a sheave at the peak of the main gaff with the fall leading
down the mast; the sheet was shackled to the clew before the sail
left the deck. This method, with the vessels shorthanded as they
were in those lean times, was by far the best. The *Garlandstone*,
as I said, was a new ship, and looked it. She was kept smart and
tidy but nothing was done for show. Her halyards, sheets, and all
her running gear was, if not black, extremely dark in colour. Capt
Murdock informed me that when he bought a coil of manila he
always soaked it for at least a day in creosote mixed with another
liquid (the name of which I cannot recall) to preserve it. This may
have been profitable, but I was to find that when on a passage,

especially when wet either by sea water or rain, one's hands and forearms soon became impregnated and permanently black and later mine became affected with an itchy rash. But there was no old or unsafe gear anywhere to be found.

We left Portishead the next morning with a nice easterly breeze. At high water we shortened in the cable, hoisted the mainsail and mizzen, and speedily had the anchor stock clear of the water. Next we hauled up the jibs, and, as her head payed off the little ship heeled and forged ahead. Here, unlike the dear old *Jane*, one felt lively movement and quick response. Next we fished the anchor and got it on the rail secured with the shank chain. Then came the topsail, the first time ever I had helped set one 'flying', but the captain had already explained 'the drill' to me, and with a small amount of fumble it went aloft, whilst Capt Murdock luffed the vessel up so that the sail did not foul the peak halywards on its way. Now with the wind abaft the beam the *Garlandstone* really surged along and, looking astern at the wake in the smooth water occasioned by the off-shore wind, it showed straight and true: a ribbon of white. No loose foot to the main and mizzen sails here as in the trows; both of these sails had patent reefing gear so the foot of the sails were laced to the booms, thus trapping the power of the wind that would otherwise have been lost by the down draught escaping between the loose foot and the boom.

Soon, leaving the high ground of Walton Bay and Clevedon Hills we were abreast of the low flat lands of my native Kingston Seymour. With the aid of the ship's binoculars I could see my homestead four or five miles to windward. We felt more wind from that low and open shore. Now I was at the wheel; the little ship seemed to me to be racing along, yet such was the balance of the vessel's rig there was very little effort needed to keep her on her course. The exhilaration of that first sail in the *Garlandstone*, with a smooth sea and plenty of wind, in waters I knew so well can still stir my blood nearly six decades later, yet it is tempered with regret that I shall never see, or feel, the like again. If I appear to be a little too enthusiastic over my new ship, it must be remembered that I had only recently left the oldest British registered sailing vessel then afloat and working (when work was available) on her was not easy. This was the *Jane* that was at that time 120 years old. Built at Runcorn in the year 1800, she was what was known as a Liverpool flat, but this design is so similar to a Severn decked trow that when she was sold to Bridgwater over half a century later she passed as a trow. Built of English oak she ended her days as a lighter in Bristol Docks and was broken up in 1938. Now here was I on board what was the youngest vessel on the British coast, built purely as a sailing vessel on the River Tamar less than 20 years before. She was to me a thing of speed and delight; yet the ugly *Jane* will always be my first love.

As we were leaving 'Posset' that morning (this was the name we always called Portishead) the *Via*'s boat was coming off from the shore; maybe some urgent message or telephone call. Later we had seen her setting her sails, and now looking astern I saw her considerably nearer. Capt Murdock was amused at my surprise. Here was I thinking we had the 'fastest' ship afloat and we were being rapidly overhauled. This was an object lesson for, as my skipper pointed out, with the wind abaft the beam, a schooner's topsails serve their best purpose; squared to 'fit the wind', and being so far forward in the ship, their pulling power was enormous, always providing the gear was good. Beating to windward the *Via* would not have caught the *Garlandstone*, but that day she slowly gained upon us, passed us and drew ahead, powerful and purposeful, her masts and spars scraped and oiled and gleaming against the white canvas of her sails. A beautiful picture to behold – and to recall. On that ebb we were abreast of the Nash Point by low water, but the wind held and sailing over the flood we were nearly to the Scarweather lightship by high water.

The wind fell away then and soon we hardly had steerage way; still we drifted with the ebb on our way. There was no mention of starting the engine; we were truly a sailing vessel and I was happy for it to be so.

One thing I could not get used to was the skipper's bowler hat, it seemed so out of place. I kept comparing it with the jaunty peaked cap of Capt Smart, together with his gold earrings and ruddy face.

On the next ebb, sailing and drifting, we reached the Helwick lightship; then the wind freshening from the south we were below the St Govan lightvessel by the next high water. This amounted to approximately 90 miles in one day's sailing. About a third of this time there was little or no wind, but this fortunately was mostly on ebb tide. The skipper appeared to be quite satisfied; he had not used any engine fuel.

During the next 24 hours we had variable winds from south and west and logged 90 miles on our course, which was about west. This was the first time ever I had ever been out of sight of land – in clear weather. Twelve hours later, when I relieved Capt Murdock at the wheel at midnight, we thought we could see the loom of the light on the Old Head of Kinsale. Before my watch was finished

I could see the light itself. The wind was now southerly again and the *Garlandstone* sped on with all sail set whilst I kept the lighthouse with its flashing light fine on the starboard bow. What a difference this was to me. No hard running tides here to worry about or the numerous shoals of the upper Bristol Channel. Here about there was hardly any tide to cause concern, but, to me, there was an unfamiliar motion, a slow and mighty heave quite apart from the billow caused by the breeze that blew. Capt Murdock said it was the heave of the western ocean not now so far away.

In the *Garlandstone* it was the rule to allow the third hand, or 'cook', to have all night in, so that he could be around all day to prepare the meals, and to carry out any necessary chores about the decks – or below. We were therefore still only two-handed except there was extra help to be called on when really needed, which was seldom during his sleeping hours.

At 5 am that morning during my watch below, hearing shouts, I went on deck (we never really undressed when below when on a passage). I saw a boat, pulled by four men at the oars; they were then about a cable's length away. We eased the jib sheets and luffed the vessel into the wind to enable the boat to come alongside. These four men were the 'hobblers', as we called them, from Courtmacsherry and here they were quite ten miles off-shore, there to make certain they 'spoke the vessel' first and for so doing be entitled to the work of discharging the cargo. We then heard that the *Via* had arrived late the night before and was now in the outer harbour. We had lost sight of the *Via* somewhere off the Smalls and had expected her to be ahead – with her big square topsails and great mainsail, and no propeller under her stern to help drag her back. Two boats had put off from Courtmacsherry the afternoon before, but the other boat had won the race for the *Via*. Even in the darkness it had been quite simple; seeing the navigation lights of a sailing vessel far off, the boats would each show a hurricane light and pull towards her, and the schooner's captain, seeing the lights, would know what they were and would steer as far as he was able towards them.

Our hobbler's boat had lost the race, but hearing we were not far astern had waited all through the night. This procedure by the hobblers was not unusual. When a vessel left a Bristol Channel port loaded for one of the small harbours in Southern Ireland the shipbroker (who had chartered and conducted the business of the ship) would send a wire to the broker in the port of discharge, stating the time the vessel had left the loading port. The word would then be passed to the hobblers, and they, being mostly

seafaring folk, would estimate, according to the weather prevailing
(as far as they knew) how long the ship should be on passage. They
knew both the shippers and their vessels and judged accordingly.

The hobblers chided Capt Murdock for having stayed at Portishead for a whole day, and not just one tide which upset their
calculations. The captain looked embarrassed (for he was known
as a man who got around!) but I knew the reason – having a new
mate aboard and a young one, a night departure from that anchorage in the narrows of the channel may have been imprudent. For
this I blamed him not at all. I felt he knew by then he need not
have worried.

To come back to the hobblers, by now Jack the cook was about
and he quickly made a huge jug of cocoa and buttered some ship's
biscuits with good Irish butter. Those men were in patched and
ragged clothes; they were cold and shivering and without a smoke.
They sat in the galley and enjoyed the luxury of the fire in the
range. They had been in their boat, just an open boat, for about
fifteen hours. The amount they would receive for shovelling the
coal out of the *Garlandstone*'s hold would be four pence per ton
for her cargo of 120 tons – two pounds – between them, but usually
there were three men in the team. That was the rate for the job in
Southern Ireland in the early 1920s. Capt Murdock did not tell me
what freightage he was getting, but I well know that in the late
1920s the rate per ton for a cargo of coal from Lydney to Courtmacsherry was six shillings per ton.

As we sailed into Courtmacsherry Bay to the south west of the
Old Head of Kinsale, Capt Murdock went below and prepared his
engine for when it might be needed to enter the harbour. The
hobblers, seemingly ready to please and certainly knowing 'the
drill', got the anchor off the rail. We got the topsail down and
stowed below. With a roar from the 'engine room' the engine
started and with so much willing help from the hobblers the sails
were quickly lowered as we motored into the harbour. This was
my first sight of the Emerald Isle and I was pleased with what I
saw. We had been just over three full days from Portishead, and
lucky with the weather.

Whilst on passage Capt Murdock told me that a few trips before,
whilst on passage to Waterford, the mate who had been in the
Garlandstone for quite a time had been overcome with fumes
through some leak or throwback from the engine and, when Capt
Murdock went below to see why he had been so long away, the
mate was dead on the sole of the cabin – or engine room. I understood the mate was buried in Waterford. I found afterward that

whenever we were in Waterford Capt Murdock always went to church should we be there on a Sunday morning. He also told me that a year or so before, whilst the *Garlandstone* was in a south of Ireland harbour, I forget which, four men came aboard one night with masks on their faces. Tying a rope around him they led him to some nearby woods and wound the rope around him and a tree, but leaving his hands free. The men were armed and, in the darkness, he waited for the volley to come. Some minutes passed (or so it seemed) then unable to bear it any longer he managed to reach down and grab some stones he could feel by his feet; then screaming out that he would 'smash their heads in' (such was his desperation) he hurled the stones to where he thought they must be. But still there was not a sound; then by working the turns of the rope around until he could reach the knot he untied himself and ran back aboard. Although he told the Civic Guard (Irish Police) nothing ever came of it. I understood he never again took a cargo to that particular harbour.

Years later, when I told this story to a master of a schooner I was in, and who had carried cargoes for both sides of the (then) fighting forces, he laughed and said, 'Poor old Andrew! He was always becalling the Republicans, and they did that to learn him a lesson!' The fact that the marauders did not tie the captain's hands seemed to bear out this explanation. But certainly Capt Murdock never thought this. What he told me he believed: he was a truthful man.

Another thing he advised me on during that my first trip across the Irish Sea had some bearing on the story. My oldest brother was wounded during the Battle of the Somme, and whilst on leave had left his military overcoat behind – Somerset Light Infantry buttons and all! I took it with me in the *Garlandstone* for use whilst at the wheel. 'Whatever you do,' Capt Murdock said, 'never let that coat be seen in Ireland, even by a hobbler. Always keep it safely below!' Had it not been for that overcoat I doubt if ever he would have told me about the episode in the woods. It could well be that the men who trussed up Capt Murdock for the sake of their cause, were the great grandfathers of some of the men who today carry on that fight in Northern Ireland. Enough of politics! Back to the ship.

Discharging the cargo of coal at Courtmacsherry was somewhat easier in the *Garlandstone* than any I had known before, for here we had a motor winch. This was even then a somewhat old-fashioned Petters engine with two large flywheels and a horizontal single cylinder and an exposed connecting rod and big-end. Beside it and fixed to the deck was a tall round water tank that, I suppose, held about 60 gallons to cool the engine. I recall there were sundry glass cups which had to be kept full of lubricating oil, and from these the oil dripped on to different moving parts of the engine. This innovation was a wonderful thing, for it replaced the dolly winch (although the latter was still aboard) in lifting the cargo out of the hold. It drove a shaft set athwartships with a barrel at either end – like two small capstans on their sides. Instead of the tail of the wire cargo whip being attached to the dolly winch which was manually worked, a manila lanyard was attached to the whip and, with the motor winch running, the winch-man had only to have one turn of the lanyard on the barrel of the winch (it was actually a turn and a half) and by pulling it tight enough to grip the barrel, the basket of coal (or whatever cargo it was) was hoisted quickly from the hold. By easing his pull on the lanyard, but still with the turn on the barrel, the basket could be halted and held aloft at any height required, ready to be tipped or carried away, whilst the barrel of the winch spun around inside the turn of the lanyard. The basket, even when loaded, could also be lowered if required by the simple act of slacking the lanyard away whilst the barrel still re-volved. I well remember writing home and telling my people about this, to me, wonderful 'labour saver'. Of course, it was used to hoist the mainsail as well.

That winch must have been secondhand when it was installed in the *Garlandstone*, for I realised afterwards that it must have been worn out. The cylinder being horizontal had suffered wear at the bottom by the years of working and the weight of the piston, which was about six inches in diameter. This allowed the gases to escape from the cylinder over the top of the piston, thus forming carbon which, if allowed to cool, became as hard as concrete, so that it was nearly impossible to start the engine. Immediately the cargo was out therefore, and whilst the engine was still hot, the piston had to be withdrawn, scraped clean of the gummy carbon, oiled and replaced. Even if we left it an hour whilst we had a meal, it made the work hard and irritating. Capt Murdock introduced me to that messy exercise immediately the first cargo was out. One had only to remove the bolts from the 'big end' and the piston could be withdrawn, with the help of a tommy bar. Then using three long and thin table knives, kept for the purpose, the three rings of the piston could be slipped off by inserting the knives beneath them. Then one had only to remove the carbon from the piston and the grooves which accommodated the rings, oil, and reassemble. But it took an hour, and after a long day's work, especially if it was cold and wet, and after dark with only an oil lamp to work with, it was a very unpleasant chore.

Writing of oil lamps reminds me that in those days at Court-macsherry the lamp lighter would ride along the quay on his bicycle when evening came carrying a ladder on his shoulder. At each lamp post he would dismount, put up his ladder, go up and open a pane of the lantern and put a match to what must have been an oil lamp within – trimmed in the morning when it was extinguished – as I imagined they did in Dickens' day. But even that was progress compared to where I was born in Somersetshire where the nearest street lamp was over three miles away.

Before we had discharged the coal at Courtmacsherry, Capt Murdock was lucky in getting his vessel chartered to load a cargo of oats, in bulk, from Bandon to Gloucester, his home town. It may not have been all luck, for he was known to make quick passages and that, of course, meant that merchants and brokers and all others concerned, got paid more speedily. Bandon is some miles up the River Bandon and the mouth of that river discharges into Kinsale Harbour. I forget whether or not we motored from Court-macsherry to Kinsale; it is not far. But we certainly had to motor up to the market town of Bandon which, I believe, is about six miles inland. Here we brushed out the hold and prepared to receive the cargo. We were three days loading the *Garlandstone*'s cargo of about 80 tons (that was all her hold could accommodate of so light a cargo), the reason being that the complete cargo was brought to the ship from the farms, or small holdings, some near and some far inland, by horses and carts; some of the carts were drawn by donkeys. None of the vehicles carried more than a few hundred-weight, so there must have been well over 100 horses (or donkeys) and carts. Recounting this over 50 years later, I cannot recall how each load was weighed, but weighed it was somewhere on the quay, and the 'checker', recording each man's load as the sacks were emptied down a shute into the hold, had many altercations with the farmers when the latter disputed the number of bushels he was being credited with.

As the oats piled up in the hatchways, we the crew had to trim the load back under the decks with huge 'number 10' shovels until the hold was level full. This was the moment when Capt Murdock, now wearing a boiler suit and still his bowler, produced three worn-out deck brooms from which all the bristles had been cut away. Jumping down into the oats in the hatchway with one of the brooms – he'd given us the other two – and lying flat, he wiggled away under the decks calling upon us to follow. Then

working from amidships (lengthwise) and using our hairless brooms
the three of us pushed the oats out to the sides of the vessel so that
it piled up between the beams, driving it so hard that it was forced
firmly up tight to the decks. Those athwartship beams were seven
inches deep and, owing to our struggles and our weight, in the
confined space, it was surprising how the cargo seemed to shrink
and how much extra cargo space we made through the middle of
the ship. But it was one of the most soul destroying jobs I ever
had to do. To make matters worse it was during a heat-wave.
Those oats seemed to be able to work their way through one's
clothes, burrowing like ferocious insects, reaching the most unlikely places and there, aided by the perspiration, would prickle
and tickle to a maddening degree. The *Garlandstone* had very small
hatchways for she had been built to go, and stay at, sea (unlike the
huge hatchways of the flush deck trows). Working as we were
therefore, close up under the deck, choked and stifled by the dust
we really suffered. Capt Murdock although then an elderly man,
was a real man, and did his full share of the work, and by example
stifled any complaints that may have been forthcoming. We
crammed her brim full, battened her down and washed her down,
glad to be free of the chaff-like dust.

We motored down the river to Kinsale Harbour and, as it was
now blowing hard from the westward and the sky, looking wild
with darkness coming on, the captain decided to stay in the harbour
for the night and get ready for an early start in the morning. This
enabled us to hoist the boat aboard and gripe her well down on the
main hatch. The loading gaff was securely lashed beside the bulwarks, and everything loose either put below or made safe from
tumbling about and plenty of time to do these very necessary jobs
instead of the usual last minute scrabble.

My recollections of the River Bandon are extremely vague. It
could not have registered itself in my mind, and yet supper that
night in Kinsale Harbour stands out bright and clear – it was cold
pig's head, hot potatoes and swedes, with huge slices of bread and
Irish butter. The heat-wave had been replaced by an unusually cold
westerly and, all our work done, down there in the forecastle with
a nice fire in the fireplace and the warm glow of the gimbled lamp,
tired as we were we relaxed and ate our fill and listened to the
whine and hum of the wind through the shrouds and stays of the
mainmast not many feet away. And then – 9 hours in the bunk!

Next morning we had breakfast at six. It was a very wet and
windy morning, but the barometer was no lower than the night
before and it was a fair wind, about south west. We put two rolls

Plate 1 The ketch-rigged decked trow *Wave* in the early 1920's. She is ready to discharge about 100 tons of coal from Lydney at the Lympsham wharf on the river Axe, Somerset, for a freightage of £15.00. Road transport today from Lydney would be around £200.00. Photo: Basil Greenhill & Ann Giffard

Plate 2 Three masted schooner *Nellie Fleming*. The schooner, with the tug boat seen hanging on to Lydney pierhead, is waiting for the tide to ease. The tug will then tow the vessel to Kingroad, where she can make sail with room to manoeuvre. Photo: National Maritime Museum

Plate 3 (top right) Gloucester ketch *Isabella*. It happened all over: ships which had supported families for generations could not compete any more. Unwanted, even for breaking up, they were hidden away in muddy creeks and left on beaches, the victims of progress. Photo: Grahame Farr

Plate 4 (bottom right) Trows *Ark* and *Fanny Jane*. The two vessels appear not to be sailing anywhere seriously, but 'hanging about', waiting for water to change berths, hence the indifferent setting of the sails. The men in the ship's boats may be 'hobblers' waiting to take the mooring ropes. Photo: National Maritime Museum

Plate 5 The ketch *Lily*. This picture of the shapely little vessel, taken years before I was in her, shows her in the same berth at Lynmouth where we discharged the coal in the 1920's; In those days she had a tiller, afterwards a wheel. Photo: National Maritime Museum

Plate 6 Coasting ketch *Garlandstone*. Sailing vessels waiting in harbours to discharge or load could not avoid untidy appearance owing to so much cordage and gear having to be clear of the stevedores. Here, the little ship looks exceptionally so – evidence of change of ownership. Photo: Grahame Farr

Plate 7 The coasting ketch *Garlandstone*. This picture shows the vessel, her sails loosely set, presumably to dry them out. A pointer that she was no longer owned by Capt Murdock is that she had no staysail boom. If the ketch had been in his hands, the anchor would have been safely inboard. Photo: National Maritime Museum

Plate 8 (right) Coasting ketch *Garlandstone*. This picture shows her masts and topmast to the best advantage. Note the chafing gear. *Garlandstone* has been purchased by the National Museum of Wales. She will be restored to her original trading condition at Porthmadog for public viewing. Photo: National Maritime Museum

Plate 9 (overleaf) Severn trows: *Gloster Packet*, *Providence* and *Oliver* at Bridgwater, Somerset. A common sight in the first two decades of this century. Providence discharging coal, the others being repaired. Note the horse and cart – a sight to recall! Photo: National Maritime Museum

Plate 10   Ketch *Thomasine and Mary*. This picture came to light after the story of the loss of the vessel was written. Despite the heavy battering she had to endure her masts are still standing. Evidence of our standing rigging overhaul. From an old newspaper photograph

Plate 11   Ketch *Thomasine and Mary*. In this picture of the wreck the companion way to the cabin can be seen facing aft. The tiller can be seen jammed on the rail – when the vessel's papers were being retrieved the swinging tiller had to be avoided. From an old newspaper photograph

Plate 12 Three-masted schooner *Mary Jones*. This stalwart old ship was built for the Newfoundland trade. It was easy to imagine her in her young days standing up to the ferocious north Atlantic. I had happy times in her with Capt Shaw and the Irish crews. Photo: National Maritime Museum

Plate 13 (top left)   The trow *Palace*. When writing about the *Palace* I had no knowledge this picture existed. She looks as I described her 'shabby and bluff bowed'. She has brought stone to the shore adjacent to the berth where her parting rope caused me disfigurement. Photo: National Maritime Museum

Plate 14 (bottom left)   Sloop-rigged open trow *Nellie*. This picture, taken by my schoolmaster, shows her discharging stone on the north Somerset coast. The author, aged 10, is sitting on the gunwale. Others are:– Thomas Eglinton; Oliver Clark; Jim Simms, the mate; W Stone; Jack Clark; Capt Rowles; W Rowles. Photo: Author

Plate 15 (above)   Here, as a coal hulk, is all that was left of the ketch-rigged trow *Jane*, in 1933. Six decades ago the author thought his old ship, the first he ever sailed in, was the most beautiful thing afloat! Now her deeply carved name and her massive rudder head were all that allowed me to recognize her. Photo: Grahame Farr

Plate 16 Double topsail schooner *Two Sisters*. Here, the old ship is leaving Dover Harbour. The slack bob-stay indicates the anchor is not yet clear of the water, otherwise the bob-stay would have been bowsed down on the windlass, thus tautening the three jib stays. Photo: National Maritime Museum

Plate 17 (top right) Schooner *Two Sisters* leaving Dover Harbour, 1930. Capt Cocks is at the wheel and the author can be seen looking over the rail watching for the ring of the anchor to appear and be 'fished', whilst three men man the heavy windlass levers. Photo: National Maritime Museum

Plate 18 (bottom right) Bridgwater ketch *Annie Christian*. When I sailed in her during the 1920's she was a beautiful vessel with a jib boom over her bowsprit – a lovely vessel with a lovely name. We see her here, spars mutilated, even her name cut down to three letters! Photo: National Maritime Museum

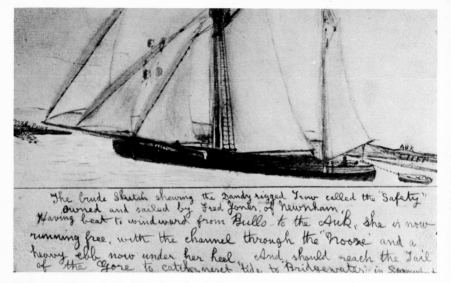

The crude Sketch shewing the Dandy rigged Trow called the 'Safety' owned and sailed by Fred Jones, of Newnham. Having beat to windward from Bullo to the Auk, she is now running free, with the channel through the 'Noose' and a heavy ebb now under her keel. And, should reach the Tail of the Gore to catch next tide, to Bridgewater in Somerset.

Plate 19 The trow *Safety*. The sketch of the trow under sail was made by Mr Joe Wathen, then 80 years old. Three men, sometimes two, could beat such a vessel laden with 100 tons of coal down the narrow reaches of the River Severn. Photo: National Maritime Museum

Plate 20 The trow *Industry*. This is a very rare picture of a trow under sail, the same *Industry* whose bottom I scraped from stem to stern in 1918 or 1919. The sail area could be halved in less than a minute. Photo: National Maritime Museum

in the mainsail as we hoisted it, and likewise the mizzen. The anchor came next and soon the stock was above the water. Next the standing jib was set together with the staysail. Meantime the captain had eased the main and mizzen sheets and took the wheel – we were away heading for the harbour mouth. Only the anchor now; but the water was smooth for the moment and the cook and I quickly hooked the fishhook in the ring and, with the burton hoisted the anchor to the cat-head, than hauling one fluke on the rail secured it by the shank chain. Next, slacking off the turns of anchor chain on the windlass and hanging them on the strong-back (a bar of iron inserted in one of the windlass bitts) we were able, by putting a couple of turns on the barrel of the windlass, to heave down the chain bobstay and belay it on the windlass where it would stay until we reached the next anchorage. This heaving the bobstay taut whilst the vessel was running before the wind sets up the wire jib stays and also tautens to a small degree the main rigging as well. This was the usual 'drill' in our little vessels, but I thought maybe somebody, somewhere, might like to read it.

By now we were rapidly leaving Kinsale astern and, leaving the shelter of the land, beginning to really feel the strength of the wind and the force of the quartering seas. It was the first time I had seen Capt Murdock wearing a south-wester. The weather forecast in the newspaper the day before told us we must expect 'vigorous secondaries, rapidly approaching from the west'. This was a term used by the forecasters in the 1920s and indicated strong blustery winds of short duration (we had no wireless reports and certainly did not have a set aboard – the only 'wireless' I had ever heard at that time was through a 'cat's whisker'). But instead here was a strong gale. However, Capt Murdock was not surprised or perturbed, for although the barometer reading was 28.50 (as we termed it) and it was steady. His opinion was that it wouldn't get any worse. 'But', he said, 'we'll have to watch it when it starts to rise', for then the wind would be likely to fly north west and blow harder for a short time. He hoped we could get to the mouth of the Bristol Channel before this happened, where we would have some shelter from the Welsh coast. This proved to be correct, and it was a lesson I never forgot. The *Garlandstone* sailed on; we had now lost all sight of the Irish coast and we were now feeling the full power of the following seas that no part of Ireland had hindered in their drift in from the broad Atlantic. To me, familiar only with the narrows of the Bristol Channel, those mighty volumes of water, galloping up astern and overtaking our little ship, was a magnificent and awe-inspiring performance. As her stern lifted high and broke through the crests of those majestic travellers there was a hiss and a roar, the surface foaming white over the deep blue of the water, the vessel seeming to slide sternfirst into the troughs whilst she was actually racing ahead at nearly 10 knots. In the troughs the *Garlandstone* looked dwarfed and puny, but we had nothing to fear, not a drop of water – solid water – came aboard. Loaded as she was with only two-thirds of the weight she could carry she had plenty of free-board, the plimsoll line being well over a foot out of the water. Jammed full to her deck-heads, as she was, with such a light and buoyant cargo, nothing could move to effect her trim; cork-like, she seemed to surprise even her master. For myself, I was amazed at such a demonstration of the awesome power of the sea, but I was glad to be there. In the many passages in later years that I made to and from Ireland, I never again experienced such an example of power and good sailing. I could now believe the many vivid stories told to me by Capt Smart whilst with him in the *Jane*! By eight o'clock that evening we thought we could see the 'loom' of the Smalls light off the port bow, showing that we had run about 100 miles in 13 hours; this also coincided with the readings of the log.

Before darkness set in we had taken three more rolls in the mainsail. Likewise the mizzen for, as Capt Murdock said, 'Should the wind increase we shall be ready'. He then told me to take the watch below, but to just lie on the locker and not turn in the bunk, and to set the alarm for midnight. Jack, the third hand, was already asleep. Having had the whole night in the night before I was not really tired. One would have to have been really fatigued to sleep during so much motion and noise, although there was a good 12 inches of pitch-pine and good English oak between my head and the gurgling and boiling water without. As the little vessel's stern lifted on the crests her stem would be buried nearly to deck level, lifting high again as the crests swept and roared ahead at twice our speed. After about an hour below I decided to go back to the skipper; on the foredeck, when I went to the bulwarks to see if the port sidelight was alright, the down-draught from the staysail was such that I felt I was being pushed down to the deck. I had never felt such force of wind as that before – it would have blown the little *Jane*'s staysail right out of her. When I got back to the captain I realised the seas coming astern were more violent than before yet the wind had not noticeably increased. In the darkness of the night the knowledge of so much water piling up, and the gleam of the stern light shining on so much white foam made me feel uncomfortable, but as Capt Murdock said, it always seemed worse during darkness.

If my attempted description of the gale force wind, the state of the sea, and the lively behaviour of the *Garlandstone* should lead the reader to think that I must have been a poor specimen to be the mate of that little vessel without having experienced such conditions before, I would point out that my lack of experience of such awesome power in no way altered my ability to handle any duty, either aloft or below I might have been called upon to do. Capt Murdock knew this, otherwise I should not have been there. The bulk of the work in the little vessels (as we called them) were they trows or craft that sailed farther afield and in deeper waters, was the 'anchor drill' and the work entailed in entering dock, harbour, or the isolated wharves in obscure rivers. It meant preparing to discharge and load cargoes, short-handed as we were and, worst of all, in the upper Bristol Channel, the navigating in the swiftly running tides and narrow fairways. We had to be alert to the many shoals and constantly changing depths of the sand-banks which abounded, handling the unwieldly trows where it was often necessary to tack every few minutes and, should the vessel mis-stay, with no room to wear, making it necessary to let go the anchor quickly to prevent a grounding and heaving it in again immediately she had canted. Tedious and really hard graft. But it developed in the crews concerned a knack of knowing what the ship was going to do before it happened. A passage to Ireland therefore in the 'wide and open' waters, in a well found and sea-worthy vessel like the *Garlandstone* was a lengthy and labour free sail.

Onward we drove before the gale, sighting more traffic now as we were getting into the narrows of the Bristol Channel. I made cocoa in the galley and we took it in turns to have a warm and a cat-nap therein on the narrow locker during the rest of the night. That night Capt Murdock told me about his schooner the *Grace* which a German submarine sank under him in the English Channel in the latter years of the war. The German commander gave them three minutes to get clear – and that included launching the boat. They scrabbled clear, but it took more than the time allotted. The commander was evidently a humane man!

Telling me of his bad passages in the *Grace* he said it was extremely rare if a topsail schooner – a well found topsail schooner – had to take in her lower topsail in bad weather; with the best possible canvas and chain sheets it did not matter even if it 'blew the moon out' (his term) – all would be well! In later years I found

this to be true. Twenty-four hours after leaving Kinsale Harbour
we were nearly abreast of Breaksea light vessel a distance of
approximately 200 miles. The wind had not eased and the barometer was still low and steady, the seas were not so far apart now
and reared more steeply than in the wider water. Daylight had
revealed a mass of white water, tumbling and menacing; gone were
the more sedate and crested beauties of the deeper water.

But all was well in the *Garlandstone*. The skipper was jubilant
for this was a quick passage. The cook had made us a lovely fry-up
for breakfast, and this we took in turns to enjoy in the forecastle.
Both Captain Murdock and myself were both red-eyed through
loss of sleep, but we were happily aware that if the wind held we
should be able, within three or four hours, to turn into our bunks
as soon as we had anchored in Kingroad. Passing the English and
Welsh Grounds lightship that morning I could see my native shore
of Kingston Seymour, and I wondered was my father watching
from the sea walls, our little vessel racing along 'all of a smother'
as he would say, but not knowing it was the vessel his son was
aboard.

We anchored in Kingroad at eleven o'clock that morning, which
was 28 hours after leaving Kinsale, a distance of about 225 miles,
an average speed of eight knots. The only sail handling we had
done was to take in the near-equivalent to a third reef when somewhere south west of the Smalls. We had made Portishead just in
time, for the barometer had started to rise and soon after we had
anchored and stowed the sails the wind came out of the north west,
but with our anchor safe in the 'Posset' mud we had no fear. One
thought kept recurring to me. It was that had the *Via* been with us
on that voyage from Kinsale, and carrying her lower topsail
throughout, the passage, providing she had been loaded with oats,
she would have beaten us easily.

More than half a century later than the passage described one has
got used to seeing, on the medium of television, young people of
both sexes sail single-handed across the Atlantic in modern fibre-
glass yachts with light man-made fibre sails, and every conceivable
navigational appliance – the modern ratchet winches for winding
in the sheets within arm's length of the person in the cockpit, jib
headed mainsails and mizzens, the luffs of which run up, and
down, in grooves in the aftsides of the masts, self-steering gear that
allows for the vessel to be left to sail on her own for hours, or
even days, whilst the crew sleeps, or attends to the many chores
that always demand attention. Our efforts in the *Garlandstone* may
not seem worthy of recording. But actually there is no comparison.

The *Garlandstone* (as were all the other 'vessels') was built as ships were a century before her time – except that she was more shapely. Her frames (ribs) would have been seven or eight inches square oak placed only a few inches apart, covered outside with planking from three inches to two and a half inches in thickness, and planked it inside with three inch pitchpine, making her sides over a foot in thickness, but her bottom was made up of stouter timbers and was probably 14 to 15 inches thick. Her deck beams would have been eight inches square oak and the deck planking two and a half inches thick. Built to take the ground when loaded with 120 tons of coal, these massive timbers were more than necessary, but the weight was tremendous.

This heavy structure needed very heavy gear to drive it along. Her mainmast from keelson to head would have been nearly 60 feet in length, 14 to 15 inches in diameter at deck level, and about nine inches at the head. The timber alone (pitchpine) in this mast weighed well over a ton. Her topmast would have been 30 feet in length tapering from seven or eight inches to about four inches at the truck. The mizzenmast would have been about 60 feet long and 10 inches in diameter at base to five inches at truck, with booms and gaffs for each mast in proportion. The bowsprit would have been around 28 to 30 feet long and 10 inches in diameter. Her main and mizzen rigging was set up with hempen lanyards rove through dead-eyes as in Nelson's day. Her main halyards were of four-inch manila, likewise the standing jib sheets; there were two other jibs. Except for her wire shrouds, her rig and all her gear was very little different to any fore and aft rig that sailed the seas at the time of Trafalgar. To handle such gear with two men and boy meant the vessel was undermanned, but the economies of the time would not allow the much needed extra hands. The shortness of the passages to Ireland and around the coasts allowed men to recuperate from the loss of sleep they suffered whilst on passage, and was the only factor that enabled them to follow their calling for the years they did.

But I digress. From Kingroad the next morning we proceeded on our way to Sharpness towing our boat astern. Using the motor, but with the main and mizzen set and the booms close aboard – for the wind was still north west. To my surprise, I found that a sailing vessel with her auxiliary engine running would enable her with her sails set, to sail much closer to the wind; her sails would draw and add considerably to her speed even when her booms are hauled in nearly amidships. Today this may be generally known; in the early 1920s it was, to me, a new experience.

Gloucester docks are linked to Sharpness docks by the Gloucester and Berkeley Canal. The canal is approximately 16 miles long
and has about the same number of swing bridges – at least this was
so at the time of which I write. Vessels with their own power could
employ a hobbler (I suppose he was classed as such) who would
need a bicycle to ride ahead of the ship and open the bridges – by
man-power, of course – and close them after the vessel had passed
through. For this service, and riding the 16 miles, the charge was
ten shillings. That huge sum amounted to nearly two days' wages
for the mate of the *Garlandstone* – or any other coasting vessel. It
had to be saved. It was simple. When coming up to the first bridge
the third hand would jump into the boat (as always, towing astern)
and make an end of a heaving line fast to the painter ring but
leaving the other end aboard. He would then scull quickly to the
bank, drop his oar in the boat and spring ashore. Some one aboard
then would haul the boat back with the heaving line and make her
fast close up under the vessel's stern. The cook – it was usually the
cook – would then run ahead, heave open the bridge. As soon as
the vessel was through, the engine would be knocked out of gear
and someone aboard would jump into the boat standing amidships
and pull her ahead as fast as possible by 'clawing' her ahead using
the ship's gunwale to bear on and drag her ahead to give her way
and, when up to the main chainplates, sheer her off and spring
aboard whilst the boat carried her way to the man waiting on the
bank. He would then jump into her and scull back aboard and
carry on with his work until the next bridge hove in sight. This
exercise would be repeated 16 times thus saving the ship 20 shillings. Such were the times we lived in. If the reader wonders why
the second man did not scull the boat into the bank to pick up the
man ashore, the reason was that the same exercise was carried out
when there was only a two-man crew – so it was the usual thing.

The amazing thing about the 'bridge drill' was that had the
Garlandstone taken a tug from Sharpness to Gloucester docks the
charge for the towage would still have been only a pound, including
the opening and closing of the bridges. The fuel the *Garlandstone*
used during the journey up the canal cost more than the cost of the
towage, but, of course, it was often a saving of time for a vessel
with her own power. During this, my first trip up the Berkeley
Canal in a motor vessel, it came about that I had to be the 'bridge
opener'. Jack, the third hand who, as before stated, had joined the
vessel a week before I did, immediately we arrived at Sharpness
had asked for his discharge. Evidently he had only sailed in tramp
steamers and ocean freighters, and he was much perturbed on the

passage from Kinsale to see seas that made the *Garlandstone* look so puny and in the night to hear the noisy slap of a sail that had for a moment or two lost the wind whilst in the deep trough of the waves. As soon as the anchor was down at Portishead he confided in me that he had thought we would have been overwhelmed. 'Never again,' he said. It was useless to tell him that one of his big old tramps, loaded to her marks with iron ore, would have been more likely to founder in that kind of sea than our lively and buoyant little *Garlandstone*, then still in her 'teens'.

Arriving at Gloucester docks the oats were unloaded by suction pipe in a few hours – quite 20 times faster than it was loaded from the horse-drawn carts. Within an hour of our arrival the shipbroker had sent word to tell the captain that a cargo of salt would soon be ready for shipment to Waterford and the charter was arranged forthwith. This was very lucky for Capt Murdock, for salt freights were always pretty high for very few coastwise vessels were tight enough to be trusted to load it. It was also lucky for the broker. For this cargo, which was in bulk, the hold had to be washed out to get rid of the dust from the Irish oats, as well as the coal dust left in the crevices from the coal cargo to Courtmacsherry. The washing out the captain and I did with hose a pipe from a fresh water tap on the dockside. It took us a day to hose down the ceiling and deck-head and scrub off with the deck brooms, and then to dry everything off with cloths, leaving all the hatches off meanwhile to hasten the process.

Capt Murdock was not very happy at having to help with the washing out owing to the absence of a third hand, especially in his home port. When I asked around the dockside if they knew of a suitable hand I met negative headshakes and covert smiles. Somewhat mystified, I pointed out the vessel was well found and there was no shortage of food. They replied that the *Garlandstone* was well found because she had to be. 'You won't lie windbound much,' they said. It was now October, and at home I had a foster brother who had left school during the last days of August. When I mentioned this to the captain, his words were, 'Is he hefty? I suppose he can boil hot water?! Pop down and bring him back Monday!' This was on a Saturday. Back aboard on the Monday I had to go ashore and buy my brother some dungarees to cover up his bare knees, as he only had short trousers. Today, nearly 60 years later, that boy is master of a tug boat at Avonmouth having spent all his working life at sea.

After loading the salt at Gloucester docks in the *Garlandstone*, no time was lost in leaving the Captain's home town and getting

down to Sharpness. I have already described the 16 bridges and
how they were operated by the vessel using the Berkeley Canal,
and my first round trip in the *Garlandstone*.

As one trip in that good little ship was very like another, there
would be no point in describing the whole voyage to Waterford in
detail. But off the Pembrokeshire coast where we arrived at midday,
the wind was gusting down from the north bringing banks of black
cloud with occasional heavy squalls of rain and hail. It was a
smooth water wind and under the shelter of the high land we were
able to carry all sail except the topsail and flying jib. As we headed
towards the Smalls lighthouse and opened up the North Channel
(as Capt Murdock called it) we felt more wind – more squalls with
torrents of hail that came sweeping down like mighty beards hanging from the sky, turning the sea seething white as they raced
along. We rolled down two rolls in the mainsail, likewise the
mizzen and took in the boom jib. The decks on the lee side filled
with hail nearly halfway up the bulwarks. My young foster brother
cleaning his pots and pans in the galley looked out in wonder when
the hail beat down on the roof, and into the mainsail, making a
terrible din. Not a very nice first trip for a boy of fourteen. The
beam sea being steep and heavy, Capt Murdock decided to turn
back to the shelter of the land. Round on to the port tack we
quickly made the lee of the high land. I had thought we may have
gone into Milford Haven and anchored snug in Angle Bay, but in
this I was mistaken. After about an hour on the port tack in the
smooth water, we put the vessel about again but kept the staysail
to windward; we were thus hove to and with the sheets hard in
only forged very slowly ahead. This 'dodging about' under the
weather shore was Capt Murdock's alternative to the comfort of
Angle Bay. He contended that once the anchor was down people
were apt to wait *too* long for the right weather. 'We've got the start
of them out here,' he said. 'We shall be away ahead before they
start to heave up their anchors!'

This confirmed what I had heard in Gloucester that we shouldn't
lie wind-bound very much in the *Garlandstone*. Of course Capt
Murdock was right. He was a good shipmaster in a well found and
sound ship. But I did not quite agree with this at the time, knowing
that other vessels bound for Ireland were lying comfortable in
Angle Bay. Bearing in mind that a sailor's month consisted of 30
days, my wages worked out at just over five shillings per day. By
sunset that evening (it was the month of October) the squalls ceased
and the wind veered to the east and eased enough for us to carry
the full main and mizzen. We let draw the bowline, hoisted the

boom jib and with the Smalls light on the starboard bow we proceeded on our way. The captain, highly pleased, said: 'Those fellows in Angle will be almost sure to wait for daylight; in there with their anchors down!'

Four hours' sail from the Smalls the wind veered to the southeast, making it necessary to jibe the bringing the wind on the port quarter. We hauled the log and the reading showed we had covered 22 miles, half way to the Coningby light vessel. The captain went below to mark the spot on the chart telling me to steer a more westerly course. Soon a thick misty rain started to fall and, as the wind was freshening, Capt Murdock decided we had better put three rolls in the mainsail and mizzen. My foster brother had long been in his bunk; having been only three days aboard he would have been no use on deck in the dark. There being only the two of us, therefore, prudence demanded that the reef was taken in early. In the early hours of the morning we hauled in the log but it had fouled itself with strings of seaweed. It showed us another 16 miles, but how long past had it become fouled? In any case we must then have been abreast of the Coningbeg light ship and Capt Murdock thought well to the south of her; we never saw her light on account of the driving mist. Soon Capt Murdock decided to bring the ship to and keep the staysail to windward. This meant the boom jib, which we had carried to ease the amount of weather helm, had to come in.

Out there in the darkness on the bowsprit I quickly made a 'rough stow' of the jib, but I only realised then from the way she was throwing her bows about how much the sea had increased. Back aboard, the captain told me to 'get the boy up on deck and put the slides in the scuttle', and to my remark of surprise said: 'When we start to round her to, shut him in the lavatory. He'll be safe there.'

When he gave the word I ran forward and put my foster brother in the lavatory, telling him to sit on the seat and bolt the door. I then ran aft to haul in the mizzen sheet as far as I was able. The captain, easing the helm, brought the vessel to the wind enough to reduce the pressure on the mainsail, thus allowing me to haul in the four-inch sheet of that sail and bring the heavy boom in to the rail; otherwise one man could never have managed it alone.

This done I ran forward again to attend the jib sheet. Came the call from aft: 'Ease up.' (Gloucester men did not always shout 'Lee-ho' before going about). I slacked away enough sheet to spill the wind from the jib; the sail slammed and thundered, the vibration of its stay being transmitted to the deck by way of the mast;

the flailing sheets of manila and chain a menace that could disfigure
or even worse. No time to lose, the little ship's bow was swinging
head to sea, the ship still forging ahead. I quickly took a turn
around the windlass bitt with the port sheet tautening in the clew
– taming the wild beast. Just then the bows broke through a crest
and dipped downward into the valley. This, of course, was the
moment Capt Murdock had been concerned about. I clung to the
turns of the jib sheet and crouched behind the windlass barrel. For
an instant I saw the reflection of our navigation lights on the sea
ahead, the *Garlandstone*'s bow reared upwards but, lively as she
was, she could not escape it all. A volume of water rose up, burying
the knightheads, tumbling aboard, roaring, gushing and squirting
over and around the windlass. I was drenched and gasping with
the cold, but at no time was I in any danger, neither was the ship.
I have described the incident merely to point out the action required
by one man when only two had to handle such a vessel, and one
of them had to be at the helm. In fine weather there were few
difficulties, but in heavy weather and dark at night it could be
unpleasant and exhausting.

Round now on the starboard tack the *Garlandstone*, her staysail
to windward – for I did not let draw the bowline – rode easily and
comfortably, even though there was plenty of lively motion. But
what of the boy in the closet? Well, it was his first trip to sea, and
in that small lavatory he was in total darkness. The four corner
posts of that structure were the only parts of it that reached the
deck where they were bolted to angle plates. The sides, front and
back were four inches clear of the deck, this enabled the deck to
be washed down as if there was no lavatory there. When the sea
came aboard however, with the lift and roll of the ship such a
volume of water found the closet an obstruction, consequently the
water boiled up inside up to the boy's knees. For all he knew the
vessel may have been sinking – a night to remember.

I have often wondered why Capt Murdock thought it necessary
to get the boy on deck. I thought to have had him out of his bunk
and dressed would have been enough. His caution may have had
something to do with the tragedy of finding his last mate dead in
the engine room, overcome by fumes some months before I joined
the vessel. He was certainly not a nervous man. It was a bad start
for a young boy. Now in his sixties he has never forgotten those
ten minutes in the closet, and the hallabaloo around him.

We dodged about from one tack to another with the staysail to
windward until dawn. We had seen no lights; on such nights,
windy with fine driving rain, no one can judge the range of visi-

bility. Only the foolish would venture too near a lee shore in such conditions hoping to pick something up.

Daylight came, and with visibility judged to be from two to three miles we kept away for the land. In less than an hour we picked up Hook Head on the starboard bow, just where it should have been. No hobblers boats out that night to greet us ten miles off, but they were waiting some distance inside the Hook. We were glad to see them, for here was willing help and we were not a little tired.

I have described the arrival of the *Garlandstone* off the Irish coast in some detail not because it was in any way spectacular; it was the very opposite. It was done every day on some coast or other, often by men who could hardly read and write and very few vessels were lost in such exercises. The navigational aids were elementary – the compass, the log and the lead (the log had to be hauled in to be read). Every tack we made that night was timed, with the necessary allowance made for the tidal streams and so arriving fairly accurately at the distance sailed over the ground. Yet at the time of writing one hears of vessels with every modern type of electrical aid – radar echo sounders, automatic helmsmen – colliding in clear weather and, like a trawler recently running on the rocks near Land's End in fairly fine weather and becoming a total loss, destroyed through being provided by those very devices installed for the safety of the ship and well-being of the crew.

The *Garlandstone* loaded oats again from Waterford to the Bristol Channel; one round trip was very much like another except that we never had to dredge up or down a river owing to her having an engine. Eventually the coal tar/creosote oil substance with which all the ropes were steeped before they were rove, got so ingrained on my hands and wrists, especially during wet weather, I acquired an itchy rash which became raw and painful. I learned later that it was dermatitis. My foster brother and I left the *Garlandstone*, saying goodbye to her in Cardiff.

Inclement weather in the Bristol Channel

I cannot recall how it came about, but I had not been at home long before I was asked to go to Appledore to join a little vessel – the *Renown*. The skipper was a Highbridge man and his name was Chapman. The two of us were to sail her by the shares or thirds. At Appledore I found Capt Chapman bending on some of the sails; the *Renown* had been laid up. I recall it was winter time in 1926, and that we kedged her down from Bideford, myself sculling the kedge ahead in the ship's boat using 120 fathom of winch line, but for this there was an extra hand aboard to keep the dolly winch going. Of the first trips we did in her I remember little. The trip that stands out is when we were fixed for a cargo of grit to Weston-super-Mare. I well remember loading the planks and trestles, with wheelbarrows etc. at Appledore quay, and getting the vessel off to the 'ridge' with the loaders aboard, and mooring her where they wanted her. I forget what pay the loaders got; it was certainly not very much, but they were a happy gang and did not take long to complete the loading. There were many little vessels laid up at that time off Appledore quay; some representing the life savings of families who were unable to afford the repairs called for after survey, there being no prospect of any remunerative trading during that very lean year, 1926.

We left Appledore the next day. The owner, Capt Thomas Hutchings, who informed us he may be able to fix us with a cargo of bricks for Dublin from Bridgwater, stood on the quay watching us get under way. Although the wind was southerly it took us four tides to get to Weston-super-Mare. We found during that time that the vessel was making a fair amount of water. The cargo of grit was for the Weston Council; it was used mainly on the roads. We arrived off Knightstone one lovely morning; there was a light southerly wind. We just sailed the vessel in within a couple of lengths of the Knightstone wall to windward, lowered the anchor, and with the help of some boatmen, quickly moored her all fours close beside the slip. I recall the Weston Council's horses and carts were soon on the scene together with a motor lorry. The cargo of course was winched out by the vessel's gear. Knightstone is not a very comfortable place to be caught in should a strong westly wind develop, so we were thankful to leave again that evening for Bridg-water to load the cargo of bricks for Dublin. With the south breeze still prevailing, we left at high water and, on the port tack, were soon nearing the east Culver buoy where we put the vessel on the other tack. Then, with the ebb sweeping her down, we edged across Bridgwater Bay and were soon at anchor north and east of Cobbler Patch just outside the mouth of the River Parrett.

I cannot recall how the arrangements were made, but a Bridg-water tug picked us up at Burnham the next morning and took us in tow up the muddy and swiftly flowing River Parrett. A pilot also boarded us, for pilotage was compulsory. Nearly 20 years later, during the Second World War I met that pilot again when I was in the Bristol barges; he was in the same firm. Three of his sons were also in the Bristol barges, also his brother, Ira Aldridge. When I was in the *Renown* Ira Aldridge was captain of that beautiful Bridgwater-built ketch, the *Irene*, but I only discovered this when we met in the barges in 1943.

We did not go into the dock to load the bricks on this occasion, but loaded the cargo from the wharf on the east bank of the river. The bricks were put aboard by a steam crane. The loaders started stacking the bricks from aft, putting the vessel down by the stern; soon we heard the cry 'there's water on the ceiling'. We told the men that this was owing to the way she was being loaded and because she had such a flat bottom. We pumped her out and soon she was aground. After this when again she was afloat we tried the pumps now and again but there was no water. We knew the reason – when grounding she had spewed the blue clay of the river bed into her bottom seams, thus sealing the leaks, but we were aware that as soon as we were out in the channel again and the old vessel did a bit of 'washing about', the respite from the pumps would be over.

I believe we loaded about 35,000 bricks, and there were 100 or so chimney pots, ridged tiles, etc. They used to say that roofing slates were the worst cargo a wooden vessel could have in her hold because when she strained and twisted (as the old vessels did) in boisterous weather, the slates would drop here and there and,

acting as wedges, prevent the seams from closing up again. Next
to slates in the list of bad cargoes came bricks, said to act the same
as slates. I should have thought that slates could have been stowed
in alternate courses fore and aft and athwartships thus preventing
the downward movement of any of the slates. There is no doubt,
however, that a 20-hole Bridgwater brick straight from the kiln
will soak up its own weight in water; some proof of this will be
seen later in this account.

When we left the River Parrett with the cargo of bricks, the wind
being strong westerly, Captain Chapman decided to make for Cardiff Roads and wait for the weather to clear, and perhaps a change
of wind to give us a slant down channel. Here we 'tidied up' and
made the little ship snug for her passage to Dublin. She had started
making water again, but it was the month of June, we were young,
we had a vessel when dozens were laid up. We could see some
vessels in on Cardiff Mud, as it was called, but could not make out
who they were. Twenty years later I learned the name of one of
them and listened to her master censure the crew of the *Renown*
for leaving Cardiff Roads in the weather we did.

After two or three days of inclement weather, the wind veered
to the north west, and as this gave us a weather shore Capt Chapman suggested we try to get as far as the Mumbles. Our stores
were not so plentiful as to allow us to lie windbound too long. By
dusk that evening we were about 12 miles below the Nash and to
the southward of the Scarweather light vessel. During the day we
had observed a ketch a long way astern; we assumed she must have
been one of the vessels we had seen on Cardiff Mud. She looked
to be a sizeable ketch but we could not identify her.

By now the wind had backed to the westward. It was a strong
breeze and inclined to increase. The ebbing tide running against the
wind was putting up quite a sea and causing our old vessel to
tumble about in a very lively manner. We were on the starboard
tack carrying everything but the topsail and flying jib; before it
became quite dark we put a reef in the mainsail.

The captain had made up his mind to put the vessel on the other
tack, which would take us across the tide into the shelter of the
Mumbles. I had been down in the cabin having first turn for supper
and was making up the fire when our old ship gave a heavy lurch
to leeward. I heard the sound of splitting timber followed by a
crash and a shout from the captain. On deck I found the mizzen
mast and sail had gone over the side – to leeward of course – and
the tide having caught the sail had forced it under the quarter of
the vessel causing the stump of the mast to be standing perpen-

dicular above the rail. This brought the vessel broadside to the sea causing her to roll in a very uncomfortable manner. The captain cut the lanyards of the port rigging for this was evidently holding the masthead somewhere below the keel and preventing the stump from capsizing away from the ship. With the boom and sail attached the mast slid below the surface but we could still feel it thumping under the bottom of the vessel. By the light of the stern lamp, which we unshipped, we could sometimes see the stump of the mast appear in the turbulent sea. It was important to get the vessel on the other tack and the drag of the mast and sail on her stern nearly achieved this by wearing her round, but all our efforts to free the sail from the rudder proved to be in vain. Turning our attention to the hole in the deck, the mast had snapped three or four feet below the deck, ripping up the deck planking and the framing around the mast, leaving a jagged hole above the hold. There was too much water washing about the decks for us to be able to try to cover the hole even if we had had the materials to do it. We pumped some water out but not much more than was usual for a given period – the bricks were taking up the water almost as fast as it washed down into the hold.

Time to look after ourselves now. We took the gripes off the boat, swung her around on the hatchway and made her fast with a stout rope made fast to her stern and belayed to the main rigging. I passed a warp around outside the lee fore rigging and led it back to the boat, making the bare end fast to the painter ring and coiling most of the bight in the bottom. We then unshipped the section of the bulwark that serves as a gangway when discharging certain cargoes. We were not too soon; heavy water was now tumbling in over the bulwarks. We stayed on the hatchway between the mast and the boat and awaited our chance. When an extra heavy lurch to leeward put the old vessel's rail under, we slipped the stern painter, gave the boat a mighty heave, and she slid down with her bow through the gangway. She hung there as the ship rolled back to windward, but with the next roll back we gave the boat another heave and jumped in the stern as she floated through the gangway, her bilges clear of the rail. I slacked away the bow warp that served as a painter and we were free, and glad to be free, riding safely under her lee. We had not long to wait – in less than half an hour the old vessel gave her last roll and was gone. I cut the bow warp at that very moment.

Things looked different now; viewed from our puny boat the seas looked awesome, for the wind had freshened still more, and the fresh light of dawn showed a threatening sky.

We stepped our little mast; I hoisted the tiny lugsail but put a reef in. The skipper with an oar over the stern keeping the Nash light on the port bow, we were away before the wind. I suppose it must have been flood tide by that time, otherwise we should have made for the Mumbles. The most vivid thing I recall about that early morning in the open boat was that it was bitterly cold. If one is talking, or even thinking, about that little adventure around Christmas time, it is hard to believe that it occurred during the month of June. We drove up the channel in our little craft. She had the copper buoyancy tanks, as regulations demanded; nothing much to bother about there! But from her low level, the seas piling up astern made her appear, and feel, more puny than she was. We hauled our wind to take a look in the back of the Nash thinking there may have been a place where we could land, but found steep and tumbling seas and, farther in, a seething mass of white water. No place for us there.

After passing Breaksea Point we edged in again for the shore where it appeared to be low and likely to have a flat beach. As we got nearer in, the sea again became uncomfortably steep, but it was too late now to do anything but keep the boat's stern to those rearing heads of white water. Nearly a cable's length from the shore the boat broached to the filled. We both clung to the thwarts and within a few minutes she struck the beach and rolled over; we let go and were swept up the beach. It was a beach of large pebbles mostly shaped like rugby balls. We sat on the sward under a sea bank and we were glad to be there, for we were benumbed and winded.

The sea bank reminded me of our sea bank at Kingston Seymour. Over the bank there was a field, but the land was much lower than the saltings to seaward; again like Kingston Seymour. Nearby there was a man cutting thistles with a scythe; he looked startled when we called to him asking where we were. I suppose appearing as we did so suddenly behind him, the water running out of our clothes, shaking with cold, looking wild and unshaven was enough to startle anybody. He told us we were in Aberthaw and about three miles below Barry. We told him to salvage the boat if he could. I never heard whether he did or no. I cannot recall how we got to Barry; we had been six or seven hours in the open boat in addition to our night of trouble, but I recall the unbearable feeling of weariness and the chafe of wet clothes. I remember too having some hot food at the British Sailors' Society, or the Missions to Seamen in Barry – one of them must have paid our railway fares home, for we certainly had no money.

Twenty years later when I was in the Bristol barges, I met Capt Ira Aldridge, who was also the master of a Bristol barge, and, talking of the earlier days and the ships we had been in, I mentioned the *Renown* and her loss; he told me he well remembered it. 'I was in the *Irene* at that time,' he said. 'We were lying snug in on Cardiff mud and saw the *Renown* anchored off in the roadstead.' He then went on to say that seeing the 'old *Renown*' get under way he felt he had to follow. He said they got as far as the Mumbles but had had quite a 'drubbing'. 'You should never have left in that old vessel,' he said. If we'd had money and a full locker of food, we certainly should not have left in such doubtful conditions, but after all it was June and a quick improvement would not have been unusual. It was the economic conditions that prevailed in those hungry days where a crew of two was all that could be afforded in a vessel carrying a cargo of 120 tons, and even then if a quick passage could not be made the crew would finish with barely sufficient to afford even the most frugal provisions. Looking back now after over 50 years it seems unbelievable.

The wreck of the Thomasine and Mary

The year 1926, the year of the general strike when most of the little vessels were idle, was not a very happy year for me, neither was it a prosperous one. I have just related the loss of the old *Renown* in the early part of that year. A few weeks after that unfortunate episode, Capt Chapman came to see me. He said he had the chance to take charge of the little Appledore ketch the *Thomasine and Mary* and would I go with him? I declined, pointing out the strike was still on, and that I had a job on the sea walls anyway. But he persisted, saying the vessel wanted fitting out first of all and the owner was prepared to pay us a 'standby' wage to clean the ship up, tar her round, etc. He said we could always take a cargo of grit (Bideford grit) to Gloucester and by then the strike could easily be over. There would be plenty of coal freights then, he said, and we'd be ready and one of the first to load. Well, I was only 24 years old. I hankered after the little ships. His enthusiasm prevailed, much to my father's disgust.

Arriving at Appledore five days later, I found they had already scrubbed the vessel's bottom and tarred her round. The *Thomasine and Mary* was a shapely but plump little ship, tiller steering and, as far as I can recall, had a cargo capacity of 80 tons. Laid up just off Appledore quay were two other vessels, the *Telegraph* and the *Onward*. I believe they belonged to the same owner but the *Thomasine* seemed in the best condition; that is probably why we had her. In the sail loft were the sails belonging to all three vessels. We switched two jibs of the *Thomasine*'s which were doubtful, for one from each of the other two vessels. No one seemed to notice!

When I went aloft to hook on the two peak halyard blocks for the mainsail, I found one of the eye bolts which were bolted through the masthead, and had an enormous eye to accommodate

to hook of the block, wanted renewing, for the eye was too thin
to be safe. This meant backing out the 11-inch bolt to renew it,
and to do this we had to lower the topmast in order to be able to
use the hammer to back out the bolt. The blacksmith Jack Lamey,
the owner's brother, quickly made another bolt, dipped it in Stock-
holm's tar and and I took it aloft and fixed it. There was no need
to renew the nut; I re-used the old one. Little did I think that in
less than two years hence I should come across that bolt again in
my native village and recognise the nut.

Before we bent on the sails we cleaned up the booms and the
bowsprit. The latter was painted 'mast' colour (a kind of buff).
While the topmast was struck we had cleaned that up too, and with
a new 'pudding bag' streaming out from the truck our little vessel
looked something to be proud of. There were so many things to
attend to after a vessel had been laid up for some time: the scales
of rust and the rusty water in the fresh water tank; the flue and the
inside of the cabin firegrate, also the blackleading of the outside;
the bunks and the drawers and food lockers in the cabin; the anchor
chains to be hauled up out of their lockers and examined – a
multitude of unpleasant jobs that, if you weren't zealous enough
to find pleasure in doing them for the sake of the ship, then you
should not have been there. The crew before us had left everything
rather unsavoury, even the crockery in the lockers unwashed.

Came the day when we took planks, trestles and wheelbarrows
off to the ridge. The hobblers wheeled the famous 'Bideford grit',
as it was called, aboard whilst we, the crew, trimmed it and the
next day we sailed out over the bar bound for Gloucester. The
Gloucester County Council used the grit for the road surfaces.
Light and fickle winds plagued us on our way up the channel. It
was summer weather, and for one ebb we anchored in Lynmouth
Bay. One high water, hoping to reach Portishead pool, the wind
died away again forcing us to anchor just ahead of the Clevedon
Flats buoy. It was afternoon, windless and sunny and, although
we knew Clevedon pier was quite a mile away, it looked to be
alluringly near. We had been drifting about so long we had run
short of bread and cigarettes. This meant that although we hoped
to reach Portishead on the next flood, it would be three o'clock in
the morning. I decided to pull our boat into Clevedon Pier for we
had nearly three shillings between us. The skipper hauled the boat
up (we had put her over the side when we anchored) and put two
paddles (small oars) in her, for the distance was too far to use the
sculling notch, whilst I had a wash – for I was well known in
Clevedon at that time.

The ebb was by then running out at about three and a half knots an hour. My plan was not to put the boat athwart the tide but to keep her head upstream with the bow angled slightly towards the shore; she would then sheer herself across the stream with little or no sternway.

I jumped down into the boat, the skipper let go the painter, I quickly coiled it neatly in the bow and turned to ship the rowlocks. I then realised I was in trouble – the holes in the gunwales to accommodate the rowlocks were *not opposite* but staggered from one thwart to the next so that one oarsman with one oar only sat on each thwart (we termed this the 'lifeboat way'). As I have stated in previous chapters, most of the boat work necessary – and there was plenty – to moor or unmoor, run kedges off etc., for our little vessels in harbours or rivers, was carried out by one man sculling the boat with an ash oar in the sculling notch in the transome. I suppose the theory was that if the boat had to be pulled, it would only be for longish distances where two men should be aboard. A lot of schooners' boats had the rowlocks staggered – two men could then put the master ashore when their ship was anchored out in some roadstead, or other such circumstance.

In a very short space of time the ebb tide had swept the boat too far away from the ship forume to attempt to get back aboard, so I shipped the oars in the staggered rowlocks and, sitting sideways on the aftermost thwart with one leg the aft side and the other the foreside, pulled away like a crab with one claw longer than the other. I estimated I was losing a third of my pulling power. However, I found I could nearly hold my own against the stream whilst the tide sheered the little craft across towards the shore. Soon, by the twisting and screwing about, my bottom was sore. Time to try standing up facing forward, pushing at the oars, but this was more tiring, and the sun beating down, I began to feel exhausted – better a raw bottom. Unable to quite hold my own against the unrelenting flow of water out of the Severn, for my arms were feeling the strain, I reached the edge of the shore just below Wains Hill – about a mile below the pier. Nevertheless, my troubles were over. By using the slack water and back eddies close to the rocks, for the water was calm, in just over half an hour I was tied up at the pier. Not without discomfort, I walked up the pier, had a drink at a stall and sat on a seat from where I could see the *Thomasine and Mary*. How I dreaded that awkward and painful pull back aboard!

That afternoon I purchased two loaves of bread, half a pound of butter, a pound of sausages and 30 cigarettes for under three shillings. It was of no use to start the pull off to the ship before – or just before – low water, so I sat on the beach which was full of holiday people, the motor boats doing good business with short trips off the shore.

Later I saw a tall gentleman with a long white beard approaching. It was Capt W Rowles who was master and owner of the trow *Nellie* when she used to bring cargoes of stone to the sea walls in my very young days. A photograph of the *Nellie* discharging a cargo at Kingston Seymour is in an earlier chapter of this account. My father and Capt Rowles were friends and had sailed together in another vessel owned by the Rowles family. The old captain was highly amused at my tale of woe. 'Trust those old "Barmen", ' he said, 'to have boats different to all others!' (By 'all others' he meant trows' boats – their rowlocks were *always* opposite so that one man could pull the boat ahead to cant the vessel.)

Capt Rowles' motor boat, worked by his sons, was one of those on the beach that day. That evening they got enough passengers for 'an evening trip off to the Clevedon Flats buoy', so my troubles were over. The old captain had arranged that long trip especially for my benefit, but he would not admit it. That gave me more pleasure than the knowledge that I didn't have the long pull out. They towed me right out to the ship. The flood had started to make by the time I got aboard. The skipper had already hove the slack chain in short, thus ensuring the ship would break her own anchor out on the rising water. He could then have set the mizzen and a jib or two hoping to fetch in nearer Clevedon to save me the long pull out. But the tow out had saved all that.

It being a calm evening, the only wind we had was that caused by the flowing tide as it swept us to eastward. It gave us enough steerage way to avoid the buoys, and it was only six miles to Posset pool.

I had never been in a tiller steering vessel before. It is very handy in a small vessel; a touch of the helm and one got instant response. Sailing up the Severn the next day with the wind south-east in beautiful sunny weather was more than compensation for the bit of bother I had experienced the day before with the rowlocks – and that was my own fault anyway, for not thinking to examine a strange boat.

Arriving at Sharpness we had to tow up the Gloucester and Berkeley Canal. That canal is 16 miles long, and the 16 hand-operated bridges which span it were open and shut by a man who rode ahead on a bicycle – for that he was paid ten shillings. I know we loaded a cargo back from Gloucester over the bar. I believe it was either cow cake or fertilizer for Bideford.

Then again we loaded grit from the ridge in the river off Appledore quay, again for Gloucester. But we had no luck for a cargo
away from that lovely old port. Instead the broker there fixed us
for a cargo of barley from Portishead to Hayle in Cornwall. We
were lucky to get such a speedy fix on account of the general strike.
But Hayle was not a popular harbour to go with a sailing vessel.
Not far from Land's End, it has a bar where the ground-sea can be
pretty formidable, and pilotage was compulsory. The freightage,
if I recall rightly, was not more than four shillings and sixpence or
five shillings per ton and, as barley is a light substance, our little
ship would not carry her full cargo in weight; she would hold only
about 65 tons. Her total freight therefore for such a cargo would
not amount to more than £15.00. The crew's share of that (working
as we were by the thirds) would not be more than £5.00 between
the two of us.

We arrived at Portishead on a Saturday morning, and as we were
not to load before Monday or Tuesday, it was a wonderful opportunity for me to take the Light Railway passenger train from Portishead right to the Broadstone halt in my native village – Kingston
Seymour – for the weekend.

The night I returned to the little vessel my father and mother
drove me to Portishead in a rubber-tyred trap – a pony trap. It
was about 10 or 11 miles' journey. Being then in a nice clean little
ship, I had brought with me a decent suit of clothes – shirts and
shoes to match. I also took with me a silver watch chain and seal
which my parents had given me for my birthday. They did not
approve of me taking the latter.

The two of us trimmed the barley, which was in bulk, as it was
shot down a chute into the hold. Choked and nearly blinded with
the dust, we beam-filled her by using worn out brooms as described
in a previous chapter concerning the *Garlandstone*. The night we
left the docks there was not much wind, but we felt there may be
more when we got outside and the ebb came down. Between
Portishead Point and the Newcome buoy we were suddenly sur-
rounded by a bank of fog, but that was not unusual in summertime
in the Severn estuary, yet there was no indication of fog when we
locked out of the docks. Later when we thought we must be
nearing the Welsh Hook buoy and fearing we might be swept
across it, we let go the anchor. Sometimes we thought we could
see the flash of the light on the buoy through the fog. Later we
heard what we thought was the thumping and wheezing of a steam
barge we knew, the *John*. Obviously, he had not heard our fog
bell. The *John* was probably out of Bristol and was steering a

course (which a sailing vessel with no wind cannot do). This strengthened our belief that the fog must be very local. Feeling we were too near the fairway, we shortened the anchor chain and sheered the little ship farther over to the north side of the fairway.

Immediately we had anchored we had, of course, lowered the headsails, their heads held down by the downhauls; they were never stowed in such circumstances. The main and mizzen sails we had left up hoping for a quick breeze to clear the fog bank, but these we now lowered, resigned to spend the night where we were.

We had good old Newfoundland salt cod for our supper that night and, although there was no question of getting into our bunks, the skipper took first turn to lie down, but only on the cabin locker whilst I kept anchor watch – most of the time standing in the companion way with elbows resting on the scuttle.

I called him about 2 a.m.; he made tea for us both, then I took my turn on the locker. No need to 'count sheep' to bring about sleep! After washing the barley dust off the decks and all the nooks and crannies from fore to aft, and cleaning ourselves, we were really tired for barley dust is far worse than coal dust – so that immediately I became horizontal I fell asleep.

It did not seem long before he came calling down the companion way for me to come up. I could hear much commotion above; on deck the change was frightening, the wind howling down from out the north west, whistling through the rigging and actually laying our little vessel – light on as she was – over the leeward. The short, steep seas, so close together, slapped against the port bow, the spray flying high nearly to the anchor light. We speedily got some stops around the bellies of the mainsail and the mizzen, for the fierce wind was getting inside them.

The ebb tide was still running strong, and the vessel being lightly loaded, could not have been hove up to her anchor even if we had thought of trying to get under way. Slack water not far away was our best chance. We could then, we thought, heave up the anchor and the standing jib and the peak of the mizzen would have quickly got us back to Portishead pool.

We let out some more chain even though it was getting towards low water. We also eased the fluke of the second anchor off the rail in readiness should we need it. It was very unpleasant on the fore deck, the spindrift from the vicious little seas felt like flints.

It was not long after this when our little ship gave a heavy lurch to leeward, a heavy gust laying her right over to port. Then, by her altered motion and the lessening of the noise around us, we knew she had parted her cable. By the gleam of the anchor light, we could see the chain cable leading well out from her starboard bow. This told us the chain had parted not far from her anchor. No time to lose; useless to set a jib or anything else with the burden of the dragging cable. We, with the speed of habit, let the stopper chain go on the port rail, let go the anchor, furiously paid out the chain, maybe 30 fathom; we could feel the anchor was digging in, and the little vessel rounding up – not a moment too soon for we were now in past the conical buoy on the Somerset side of the fairway.

It was then we felt that well known rumble of the chain and the anchor dragging. This usually indicates that the chain is foul of the stock, or the fluke, of the anchor. Yet we felt this could not be for, with the speed to leeward the vessel was making when we let the anchor go, it would be most unlikely for the chain to foul the anchor (returning home some months later, the local Coastguard informed me that the fluke of that second anchor had snapped off close to the crown, but we had heard nor felt nothing in that wild motion and noise). We could see by the changing light bearings – there was no fog now! – that we were quickly nearing the shore and might strike something at any moment.

It was not long before our little ship's stern struck the rocks at, what later proved to be, Ladye Point. The shock nearly knocked us off our feet. Immediately her bow swung round crashing down on the rocks broadside on. Her bilge was obviously on a ledge and, as she rolled back to seaward, a heavy surge of water swept over the bulwarks, sweeping our lifeboat, which was griped down on the main hatchway, clear of her lashings and leaving her between the mast and the main rigging. It was just then that the anchor light on the forestay was jerked out, leaving us in almost total darkness for, as we found when daylight came, we were under a low wooded cliff and no shore lights could be seen. During the first half-hour – it may have been more – we had some difficulty in staying aboard. With every lift our poor little vessel would be nearly upright, but as the sea receded she would roll back to seaward nearly on her beam-ends. The safest place was in the bow to port the fore side of the windlass where the heel of the bowsprit kept us from sliding down to seaward. But even there every time we crashed down the shock seemed to whip the topmast, for we could hear it rattle in the mast cap, the rigging twanging, giving us the fear that something could come down upon us at any minute. We could only crouch there in the darkness.

The captain, he was much older than I, was anxious concerning the vessel's log book and other papers which were in the cabin locker, the shelf locker. Also in the cabin (we both berthed in the cabin) was the silver watch chain my parents had given me for my birthday – then only two days away. I decided to go back and try to get into the cabin.

As stated before, the *Thomasine and Mary* was steered by a tiller. The arc of the tiller traversed the deck over the top of the cabin companion way. Back on the quarter deck I could hear the rumble of the rudder as it swung from side to side with the wash of the seas; I knew then that the tiller ropes had gone. This told me that with every rumble of the rudder, the tiller (a piece of oak or ash 5″ by 5″ section and about ten feet long) was sweeping across the deck in the darkness and one blow from it would easily cripple a man.

To avoid the tiller, I dropped to the deck and slithered feet first down the companion ladder. I could feel the blankets we had used on the locker whilst at anchor. They were swilling about in the water. The shelf locker was still above water and I quickly found the bundle of what I knew was the cargo book and log book etc. My drawer containing the chain was below water. The vessel lurched heavily to seaward; afraid of being trapped, I scrabbled up the ladder and keeping face down to the deck until I was clear of the tiller, lost no time in getting back to the doubtful safety of the bows. I may only have been in that cabin a minute, but it was the worst minute ever.

Soon after this it started to get light. We were able to see the loom of the cliffs and then the outline. We were relieved to see there was no stretch of water between where we had struck and the shore. Neither of us was able to swim, but this was not unusual in the vessels, and had the vessel struck some shoal further out we should never have reached the shore.

I recall it was twenty minutes to five a.m. when we were able to see the time by the skipper's watch. We could see the hatches were gone, and our boat likewise. There was barley in the surf and the ship's stern was now under water. I was the first to jump. I went out on the foot-rope to the end of the bowsprit, lowered myself and hung on by my hands and dropped into the last of a receding sea hoping to reach the bottom for a foothold. My feet must have landed between two boulders for I had difficulty in getting one of my feet clear; the next surge of water swept in over me, but I freed myself and was carried ashore and quickly scrambled clear of the surf. The captain, seeing what had happened to me, lowered himself by one of the jib sheets and let go as a sea came sweeping in. He disappeared for a moment or two, but it was a quick trip. He

discovered later he was badly bruised. My legs and ankles, owing
to being caught in the crevice, were badly skinned and I had lost
a shoe. But we were safe.

We found our way up the cliff. There was a road on the top
leading to Clevedon. I recall how very tired we were – wet, cold
and sore – but we set out to walk to Clevedon. There at the railway
station we parted, the skipper to take a train to Bridgewater (if
they would let him pay the other end!) and myself to walk to the
near village of Kenn where my brother lived. I never again saw the
captain after that day.

My parents only lived four or five miles away in Kingston Seymour but I could not face going home in the state I was. Besides,
I was planning to return to the ship at low water hoping to retrieve
my watch chain and clothes. About a mile along the road to Kenn
a motor vehicle overtook me and stopped (I had been walking on
the grass verge to save my foot); two uniformed men got out and
asked if I was from the wreck in Walton Bay. They were ambulance
men, and when I confirmed I was from that vessel they informed
me that the Walton Bay Signal Station had telephoned Bristol and
they had come in answer to that call. They had been 'driving
around looking for the crew' they said!

I refused to get into the ambulance, telling them my brother
lived only a mile along the road; they offered me a lift to his house
and I got into the vehicle. The next thing I knew I was waking up
in a very small bedroom in a nice clean bed. Sitting looking at me
were three men – they were newspapermen. They told me I was
in the Missions to Seamen's Hostel at Narrow Quay, Bristol, and
it was three o'clock in the afternoon. I was very much upset to
hear this for it was around low water and I had intended to return
to the ship at that time.

Seeing my distress, the superintendent of the home, a Mr Hol-
man, told me to stop worrying as my clothes would be ruined
anyway. He informed me that arrangements were being made to
provide some suitable clothing to replace those I had lost. This
they did the next day. But that first afternoon my head felt so
'muzzy' I had a craving for fresh air. I got out of bed, put on my
old garments – which had been dried – and went out in the streets.
In the tramway centre the news vendors were calling out about 'the
ship wrecked in Walton Bay'. I bought a paper with my last penny.
Whilst reading the account, I had a severe nose bleed, the paper
was covered in a moment. Fortunately I had just passed a chemist's
shop. I ran back to it holding the paper as a shield. In the shop the
horrified looks I received nearly drove me out again. I asked could

they help me. The chemist asked had I had an accident. I pointed to the headlines on the now tattered newspaper – my photograph did not appear until the next day. From suspicion, the atmosphere was reversed; I received only kindness. It was wonderful. The chemist told me the loss of blood was nature's cure; without it I could have become really ill. Soon after this the 'muzziness' disappeared and my confidence returned.

Back at tne Mission to Seamen, the superintendent looked relieved – so did the ship's engineer whose shoes I had borrowed. I felt they had thought I had absconded. The superintendent had some wonderful news for me. He said if I wished he could arrange for me to obtain a berth in a steamship that would be signing on a crew on 11th September, which would be three days after the incident in Walton Bay. With so many ships idle owing to the general strike, here was a chance to start again: a reprieve from destitution. I have related this because it is the reason I was never able to describe the appearance, or the state of our little *Thomasine and Mary* after the hammering she received that morning of 8th September. Many people asked me this.

Since writing this account, however, a very good friend, Sergeant Bill Knight of the Bristol Constabulary, after much trouble traced some negatives of the 50-year old photographs that appeared in most of the local and national newspapers at the time showing the little ship lying on the rocks in Walton Bay.

As a matter of interest, when I joined the steamship, I was able to draw half a month's pay in advance; this amounted to four pounds ten shillings. This was as much, or nearly as much, as Capt Chapman and myself would have been entitled to had we discharged the cargo of barley at Hayle. We had, of course, to provide our own food. The name of my new ship was the *Oxonian*. Nearly 600 feet in length, she was about nine times the length of the *Thomasine and Mary*. Owing to the strike she was forced to go to Antwerp to bunker – her bunkers held 2000 tons of coal, just about enough to take her to America and back. From Antwerp we sailed for Baltimore in the U.S.A. and loaded coal back to – of all places – Cardiff!

Sailing from Baltimore, I think it was on a Friday, after losing sight of the American shore, we were four clear Sundays at sea before we sighted the Fastnet light: 24 days to Cardiff. It was very bad weather and the ship had no governors to her screw. In the year 1858 the schooner *Alma* made a record run across the Atlantic from Nova Scotia to the Mumbles in the Bristol Channel in 14 days. She must have had wild weather too – but you see she had no screw to bother about, only sails!

I was not at home in that mighty steamship. There men talked about being in the union, and one heard the word 'overtime'. There too, for the very first time in my life, I had to put on a lifejacket – at boat drill. I hasten to point out, however, that all our little coasting sailing vessels carried all the necessary life-saving gear as required by the Board of Trade. It was our fault alone if we did not use it.

The *Oxonian* was like a floating warehouse. No skills were required such as we had to have in the sailing coasters; no cheating the wind and the tides. No friendly meals in the cabin where in its cosy intimacy after a hard passage, sundry technical points of ship handling would be discussed whereby we may have gained a mile or two and saved a tide, for the winds and tidal streams were our power and highways.

It was about two years after the loss of the *Thomasine and Mary*, when I was at home between ships my father asked me to lend a hand to erect a hay barn on a farm in our village, Kingston Seymour. Barns were mainly built of timber in this days. It was only a two bay barn, which meant it would have six legs to support it. Later, on the site I saw the six posts lying beside a hedge. Two of the posts were obviously ships' masts; looking closer I recognised one of the posts – it was the mainmast of the *Thomasine and Mary*. The peak halyard bolts were still in the masthead, one was the new bolt I had driven through to replace the old one when we were fitting the little vessel out, easily recognisable by the old fashioned nut I had reused to screw the bolt home. The farmer told me the posts had been purchased from Capt Bill Rowles of Clevedon (Capt Rowles after his retirement from the sea used to break up ships at Clevedon Pill). He had evidently purchased the *Thomasine*. Recently the writer spoke to the son of the farmer who had the barn built and was informed that the barn was knocked down two years before. The *Thomasine and Mary*'s mast had stood as a corner post for just about half a century.

The lively little Lily

I had never seen the pretty little *Lily* before she arrived at the Weston Clevedon and Portishead Railway's wharf on the west bank of the River Yeo in Somerset (now called Avon).

The Railway Company had evidently purchased her because they expected her carrying capacity of only 60 tons would be attractive to small coal merchants with limited yard space. I say this because the company had already owned the ketch *Sarah* for some considerable time, and the *Sarah* carried double the amount of cargo than the *Lily*. It was aboard the *Lily* that I first met Jack Cornish when he took charge of her for the railway company. Jack had some family connection with one time master of the railway company's *Sarah* who worked her with his two sons.

I believe Jack Cornish took over the *Lily* from one of the two sons who was formerly mate of the *Sarah*. The *Lily* when I first saw her had an auxiliary engine, probably installed by the company. But she had not been 'cut down' because of the installation. This was very fortunate, because during the time Jack Cornish and I were in her the engine *never worked*; it was rusty and neglected when we joined her. Unfortunately it took up all the cabin; our quarters, though cosy and quite adequate for two, were in the forecastle. We soon painted the forecastle, mostly white; cleaned the brass, polished the fireplace – which was also our cooking range, and finished with an accommodation to be proud of. The *Lily* also had a tiny motor winch – it was called a 'jumbo'. But this had been neglected too, it never worked, it was seized up. We put the cover over it and forgot about it. We also made sure the propeller was 'up and down' in line with the stern post, thus cutting down the 'drag' somewhat.

Both young and enthusiastic, and both liking everything tidy and clean, we enjoyed our time in the *Lily*. Even though the sailing vessels were finding it hard to make a living for the owners and crews, we in the *Lily* were at a further disadvantage owing to the management of the Light Railway not being accustomed to transport that depended, not on steam and wheels on a rail, but on the winds that blew and the state of the tides which carried their little vessels to their destinations on the beaches and estuaries.

I suppose one is apt to dwell too much on the unpleasant occurrences of life, especially if risk was involved to one's person, but in spite of the poor return for the hard labour we endured in the little coasting vessels in my early life, there were happy times too, and these most certainly outweighed the times of stress and trouble. I well remember the occasion we loaded the little *Lily* with coal from the jetties in Newport River for a merchant in Lynmouth. The *Lily* only held six 10-ton trucks, but she was a handy size for trade with the smaller merchants whose yard and purse could only accommodate small cargoes. We had just put the hatches on and battened the little vessel down when a photographer appeared on the jetty asking if he could come aboard and take some photographs of the vessel – and the crew of course. I believe the charge was three shillings for six postcard-size pictures. We agreed that if he would wait for the two of us to have a wash we would order six. I must explain here what happens when a vessel loads coal under a tip, especially if the tide is low and the ship's hatchway 15 or more feet below the mouth of the shute. A truck of coal is upended and tipped down the shute and when it hits the bottom of the hold of the vessel, an enormous cloud of dust billows up leaving a mantle of fine black powder over everything; for a few moments one cannot see a thing, and hardly dares to breathe. A few of those trucks of very dry coal and men looked like golliwogs with powdered eyebrows. We quickly had a wash and smeared some butter into our eyelids – no amount of washing ever seemed to remove the dust from the base of one's eyelids, only butter or margarine would accomplish that. Then we put on our Appledore jerseys and were ready to pose. Now the only access from the jetty to the vessel's deck was by a timber upright ladder fixed to the piles. These ladders, as the tide receded, always collected a film of salt, or sediment, but when the coal dust settled on it, it became a sort of ointment. On deck after our wash we found the photographer setting up his camera on its tripod. We'd forgotten the ladder, he was in a sorry mess, he had even smeared his face and this, with his drooping moustache, gave him the sad look of a walrus. However, he must have been a courageous and enterprising man for he was quite cheerful as he 'fiddled' about with his gear. After he had posed us and put his head under the black cloth, I whispered to Jack Cornish that I thought the old chap 'looked better when covered up'; this made us both laugh. The photographer was beaming when his face reappeared: 'That's going to be a lovely picture,' he said. 'You both smiled at exactly the right moment.' We paid him the three shillings or whatever it was for his services, and gave him the address to post the pictures to. There was no thought of distrust, not in those old days. The pictures reached us quite safely and they were good. Today I would give 500 times more than each cost to possess one of them.

I have related the story of the photographer to show how very different were the times of just over a half century ago. Poor as his pay was for his services to us, it amounted to a tenth of the sum I received when we had sailed the vessel to Lynmouth and beached and unloaded her. Even then we had not finished our commitment, for we had also to take the *Lily* to her next port of loading.

The wind being light and contrary, we had to drop the little vessel down the river stern first that evening, using her anchor on a shortened cable and allowing it to drag along the bottom of the river we called it dredging. Once clear of the mouth of the river with the wind south east we made sail and reached Cardiff Roads on the last of the ebb and let go our anchor in clear of the traffic. Here with our anchor light up we were safe for at least five hours in our bunks. We did not even tie up any sails, just lowered them down, for the weather was good. The next morning we were under way at 6.30 am and with an easterly breeze, and in high spirits we swept out past Lavernock Point and headed down for the Breaksea light vessel. By midday we were anchored in Lynmouth Roads. Here, under the lee of the Foreland, we felt hardly any wind. When we let go the anchor, the rattle of the chain running out of the hawse sounded as if we were inside a mighty drum, for the sound waves echoed and re-echoed back off Butter Hill, in what we thought was a most delightful manner. This disturbed the birds causing them to scream and squawk, but to us the quiet and peaceful scene was wonderful.

That evening the elderly pilot came off in a little skiff and suggested we go in on to the beach that evening to enable us to start early the next morning. We agreed to do this, but actually we broke an unwritten rule, which was never to spend any time on a beach, that may become a leeshore, that can be avoided. Any wind from west to north east puts Lynmouth on a leeshore. However, it continued fine and with the pilot aboard we sailed in to the mouth of the River Lyn and warped her into the berth on the beach. Here we picked up moorings that were laid for that purpose and moored our little vessel fore and aft.

That evening the 'team' that were to help us discharge the next day came down to see us. I believe they were the merchants' sons. They were about our own age and must have liked the look of us for they returned to the town and were soon back aboard again with sundry bottles of beer and a frail full of victuals. We drank, ate and sang songs, and had one of those spontaneous and hilarious evenings that are always recalled with pleasure and amusement. One wonders are those men still around? Usually when a vessel discharged her cargo on a beach using the ship's gear, the crew manned the dolly winch that lifted out the cargo, and hobblers were employed by the merchant to shovel the coal into the baskets in the hold. On this occasion however no hobblers could have been available, and, as we were anxious to be ready to leave on the evening tide, Jack Cornish and I took the place of the hobblers and let the coal merchants' lads work the ship's gear. Now digging down through a cargo of coal into a hold about eight feet deep is very laborious work, especially if the cargo contains large lumps, but once the bottom is reached the going is much easier. If the 'head' (side) of coal in the hold can be kept as steep as possible one can tilt the basket against the face and cause little 'runs' that will nearly fill the basket, thus saving quite an amount of shovelling. Men got used to the 'nack' and a surprising quantity of coal could be got out – if the winch men could keep it going.

That time the *Lily* was discharged before tea time, for there was always a horse and cart waiting as soon as one pulled away. I cannot remember seeing a motor lorry there; maybe the beach was not suitable at that time.

Well, the two of us had shovelled 60 tons of coal that lovely day at Lynmouth; we had now to get the hatches on and battened down; unrig the discharging gear; get the coal dust off our persons and prepare our tea. By this time the tide was coming around us – time to start washing down the decks. By the time out little ship floated many hogsheads had been drawn from over the side by draw bucket and lanyard, each of us taking it in turns to draw the water or scrub the decks.

The pilot was there in his skiff to help us unmoor for, you see, he had received the day before ten shillings for his services and he was well content! We too were content for there was still a light wind from the south east and, as soon as we were free of the moorings, we set the mizzen, together with the boom jib, and our little ship canted clear of the beach and we sailed her about a mile to an anchorage under the lee of Butter Hill – for soon the ebb would be running out – to await the first of the flood on the morning tide.

We had received a telegram whilst on the Lynmouth beach instructing us to return to Newport River and load coal for the River Yeo. That was very welcome news. Under way again early the next morning, refreshed and in good heart, we had a bit of bother dealing with the confusing airs and back eddies of wind under the lee of towering Butter Hill, but clear of the Foreland we had our old friend the south east breeze to help us on our way. Close hauled, with her booms aboard, on the starboard tack, with the topsail and all three jibs set, and with the flood tide under her lee, the little *Lily* really romped along.

Here Jack Cornish and I were in our element doing what we loved to do – sailing a vessel. Both of us were able to repair a sail, even put a cloth in one; sew on a leach rope; marl and parcel; use a serving mallet, and do most of the things necessary to maintain the gear of a vessel. We were able, too, to take her anywhere where ordered, yet circumstances were such that we had to shovel the coal out of her as well. We were forced to be labourers to keep the jobs we loved to do. But that morning as she foamed along up the Bristol Channel, her decks aslant, to load another cargo which we should have to shovel out in the Yeo, we were happy lads enjoying to the full the grace and beauty of our little ship as she slipped through the water, her wake astern showing straight and true.

One blessing about taking a cargo to the River Yeo was that there were no harbour dues to pay; but, of course, there were no navigational aids either. A vessel without power could not sail into the river during the hours of darkness. But on moonlight nights with the wind north west, or west north west, we sometimes managed it with very little trouble – even if a vessel touched the bank it was all fairly soft mud, with no rocks or any other such hazards, so that the ship soon floated off again. I am speaking or writing – of course, of flood tide only, we would never have attempted the manoeuvre on an ebb tide. With the little *Lily* in good weather, we would creep in over the 'tail of the bar', as we called it, when there was very little water in the river, and then, with only a couple of jibs set to give the vessel steerage way, let her follow the rising tide, as it were, for there was no point in arriving at the discharging wharf before there was sufficient water to accommodate the vessel in her berth.

The total freight for the *Lily*'s cargo of 60 tons from Newport

to the River Yeo was about two shillings and three pence per ton.
As we were working the vessel by the thirds, our share therefore
for the two of us was about forty-five shillings and this included
discharging the cargo. Today three lorries could bring the same
cargo by road, but I understand their rate per ton from South
Wales to north west Somerset (now called Avon) would be £4.00
or £240 for the *Lily*'s cargo.

As soon as we had discharged our cargo from Newport and
taken our share of the miserly freight, we were ordered to go to
Lydney for another cargo of coal for the Light Railway. We had
both developed severe head colds whilst shovelling out the coal,
but we wasted no time in getting away for the wind was southerly
and too good to be missed. It was an afternoon tide and as we
sailed out of the mouth of the river and hauled our wind, pointing
the little vessel towards Wains Hill, we were able to see my father
and his men working on the sea walls.

We had no chance of making Kingroad over the ebb tide, the
great thing was to get clear of the river whilst the wind was fair.
With a strong west or north west wind a vessel, light as we were,
could be trapped in the Yeo for a week. We anchored just below
the Blackstone Rock in the 'gut' between the Kingston Flats and
the Langford Grounds just about a mile above where I knew my
fishing poles, on which I used to hang my shrimp nets, were sited.
Here we were sheltered after half ebb, and till half flood tide, by
the various sand banks themselves from any weather from seaward,
thus giving us plenty of time to get away in smooth water should
the weather suddenly become foul. Such is the value of local knowledge where familiarity inspires confidence.

Under way again on the first of the flood we were in Kingroad
before high water in the early hours of the next morning. The wind
by now was westerly so it was a good job we had 'scrabbled' out
of the Yeo when we did.

The colds that had come upon us a day or two before were now
much worse; we felt really groggy and as soon as our little ship
was anchored just above the Firefly Rocks and the anchor light up,
we tumbled into our bunks without even a hot drink.

The next low water was about 10 am and soon after we should
have been preparing to get under way for our trip up the Severn.
We realised now however that we really had the 'flu. Robust and
strong 36 hours before, we now found our legs would hardly
support us. We paid out more anchor chain, gave the little vessel
a sheer in towards the shore, put the becket on the wheel to keep
the helm to starboard and went below to our bunks. But we took

the anchor light below with us intending to trim and fill it later, for it was most important that it was exhibited on the forestay during the hours of darkness. Meantime the weather was on the change, the westerly wind had veered to the north west and, lying in our bunks, the noisy chop of the water told us the wind was increasing. No need to worry about our anchor chain getting foul of the anchor during slack high water, for the *onshore* wind would see to it that the little ship swung well clear inside of her anchor as the ebb came down. All we had to do was alter the helm to port. When we did this (for we both went on deck, each fearing the other would need help) we also put the anchor light up – hours before time – for we felt that once we again got into our bunks we might pass out for many hours to come. Just then however the Sharpness tug *Resolute* came alongside asking if we would want a tow up the Severn the next morning. Evidently the former crew of the *Lily* used to employ them. Immediately the skipper recognised us, he knew we were local lads and did not require his services, but he kept looking at the anchor light we had put up in the afternoon! We had to tell him we were ill and might not wake up before dark and had put up the light while we were able. As it later turned out, that routine call by the *Resolute* was our salvation.

That evening after dark the wind from the north – it had veered from the north west – increased to gale force, but we were only semi-conscious, and in any case the Welsh coast was only four miles to windward, and we were sheltered till about half tide by the Welsh ground sands. In the early hours of the next morning, about an hour after high water, our little vessel dragged her anchor and was driven ashore on the Portishead mud. But the *Lily* only drew about four feet six inches of water light, so there was no heavy surf to batter her when she struck; also the mud thereabout was too soft to walk on so she could not hurt. Had the little vessel been loaded she certainly would not have dragged her anchor. Had we not been struck down by whatever virus it was, we should have been on deck in such circumstances, and a second anchor would have been let go thus avoiding the grounding. Ill as we both were, the incident added to our feeling of helplessness and brought worry to us both, but mainly to the skipper. We would imagine it going 'the rounds'. 'They put her ashore you know!' 'Asleep in that weather? Probably drunk!' No one would believe the truth.

However, there was nothing we could do, it would be ten hours before she floated again, so we gladly fell into our bunks with 'narry a drink or a bite to eat', craving only to be still, our resistance gone.

That afternoon after about 10 hours in our bunks, we got out and, putting on all the warm clothes we had, manned the windlass and as soon as the little vessel floated, tried to heave her off; there was still a strong wind. We found we could hardly lift the levers of the windlass. It was nearly two days now since we had eaten. Suddenly we heard a 'toot, toot!'; it was the tug *Resolute* – she must have come from the pier head at Portishead. Coming alongside the skipper put his deckhand aboard us, he made fast a breast rope, and steamed slowly off whilst the deckhand, with some help from us, 'clanked' in the chain. Although the tug 'broke the anchor out' we thought it prudent to heave the stock clear of the water to make sure the chain hadn't fouled it. Five minutes more we were far enough off with the anchor down again. The operation, thanks to the tug, had taken less than 20 minutes. Actually we were in our bunks before the tug left us. The tug hand hauled many buckets of water from over the side to wash the mud off the fore deck brought aboard by the anchor chain. Came a call down the companion way 'We've given her 30 fathom. See you tomorrow.' and with a 'toot' on her siren the old *Resolute* was gone.

Although there was only a strong breeze when we let go the anchor, that night the wind again came howling down from the north and our little ship dragged her anchor again (later it was proved that her anchor was not heavy enough), but she did not go ashore. This time, hearing the rumble of the chain as the anchor 'came home' (a dragging anchor often makes the ship tremble owing to the heavy chain tautening and slackening) we muffled ourselves up, went on deck and gave her another twenty fathoms of chain. The next morning the *Resolute* again came over to us and towed us off for the second time (for some reason she had not gone back to Sharpness with a tow), this time to a better holding ground in the tug master's opinion. No pay was even mentioned; we were in a bad way. In any case we had no money. If I have dwelt too long on such a simple incident it is because, when I look back to that time nearly 60 years ago, and compare it with the 'I'm alright Jack!' attitude we see so much of today, I can only marvel at the comradeship and concern shown to us by those tugboat men. I know too that Jack Cornish and I would have done the same for them. A sound reason why that 'Let's give 'em a hand' attitude prevailed in all the little coastal vessels, but was probably more marked in the upper Bristol Channel and the Severn River, was because the hazards were many, and the men who traded in those waters, however widely experienced they may have been, were alive to the fact that anyone of them, at any time, could need the willing help of others.

The weather became fine and in two or three days we began to feel better, but we did not feel hungry. I made tea but it tasted like poison. Even then our legs were like rubber. We even ceased worrying about the Railway Company waiting for our cargo, for we felt we were lucky to be alive.

By the time we began to feel hungry our bread was not edible, and, neither of us feeling able to scull the boat ashore (with an oar over the stern), we both took an oar each and pulled into the pier – like yachtsmen or steamboat men! Back on board, toast with lard on it was our only fare, it was all we wanted. Over a week without food. A couple of days later we were able to weigh the *Lily*'s little anchor and, with all the sails set except the topsail, with a westerly breeze on our beam and the early flood tide to help us along, we headed up towards the dreaded Shoots.

We should have felt more assured if the gaff topsail had been set, but the *Lily*'s topsail was tied up aloft and at Posset after heaving up the anchor and setting the mainsail we had neither the will nor the strength to climb aloft to loose it. We were taking not a little risk, for should the wind have died away neither of us could have managed the old exercise 'boat ahead'.

The current through the Shoots during a quickly rising flood tide can reach a speed of eight knots. At the narrowest part the width of the channel is only one and a half cables. With a light ship and a westerly wind we had learned from older men that the safest time to navigate that narrow neck of water was before the rocks on either side 'go to' (are submerged), for the current then is true, except for the whirlpool! If all the rocks are covered the swiftly running tide boils over the rocks (the English Stones) changing its course more to the eastward. A light vessel therefore, should the wind falter at the wrong moment, could fall away and be swept to leeward and destroyed. But that morning as the *Lily* pointed her bowsprit up towards the leading marks of the Charston Rock we had no problems weatherwise. Slipping through the water at about four knots, and the speed of the current adding another five knots to our speed over the ground, we seemed to race by the kelp covered rocks on either side giving one an illusion of speed, but a very realistic feeling of excitement. The swiftly changing panorama of the countryside ashore lit by the morning sun was a sight to behold.

Soon we were nearing the Charston Rock, time to put the helm up and ease off the main and mizzen sheets. Leaving Charston little

more than a stone's throw to port with the waters around it –
thwarted and confused by the diversion of the rock – roaring and
swirling on the same course as the ship. But this brought the wind
dead astern and, the speed of the tidal stream being about the same
as the wind, we were 'becalmed' and without steerage. Oh for the
topsail! With it she would have probably kept her steerage way.
However by putting a sweep through a washport, still weak as we
were, we managed to cant the little ship to bring her head to tide
thus giving some limited power to the rudder as we swept stern
first up towards the Chapel Rock. But passing the Dun Sands the
wider waters somewhat eased the tide, and the wind again 'overtook
the stream' as it were, allowing the sails to fulfill their purpose and
harness our only power, the wind.

Now with sufficient steerage way as we passed the Chapel Rock
we were soon nearing the Lyde Rocks; necessary now to haul in
the main and mizzen sheets to get into Slimeroad and pick up the
leading marks to carry us on to Sheperdine. I have already described
in an earlier chapter the difficulties of approaching Lydney with a
sailing vessel and the danger of arriving off the pier too early. Capt
Smart, when I was with him in the *Jane*, taught me by demonstration how to avoid some of the traps that are forever waiting to
catch the unwary.

Unfortunately, however, these 'difficult situations' are never
quite the same. Jack Cornish, the skipper, was not much older
than I was, and that morning we had a fair wind blowing in the
same direction as the tide was running. We feared we may arrive
off the pier too early. If we'd had a head wind the little vessel's
head could have been put down against the tide, thus allowing us
to time our arrival at the Lydney entrance to within a few minutes.
Old Severn men probably would have dropped the anchor with
enough chain out to act as a 'brake' to drop the vessel up stern
first, but we were afraid there may be some spur of rock, unknown
to us (the bed of the Severn is very subject to change) where our
anchor could hook on to a ledge and, so fierce are the tides, tear
the windlass out of the decks.

By sailing across the stream and making use of the eddies, we
'wasted' enough time to ensure we did not arrive too early. When
we were just below Berkeley Pill we saw a tug towing a ketch and
a barge leaving the Lydney entrance. It was our old friend the
Resolute, whose crew had assisted us so willingly at Posset. It was
good to hear the friendly toot of the old tug's whistle and the
raucous shouts of the crew asking were we better. The *Resolute*
still had a job to stem the tide – the stream seems to persist well to

the last few minutes. We sailed the *Lily* across the tide, and just at slack water sailed neatly into the Lydney basin. We had left the river Yeo just ten days before.

The Harbour Master and all his staff had heard all about our predicament at Portishead. It was natural with six trucks of coal cluttering up the rail head that they should have enquired from the tugs *Resolute* and *Primrose* if the *Lily* had been sighted. Then, of course, the Light Railway Company had telephoned Lydney most every day, 'Where was the *Lily*?'! Looking back to those events of over 50 years ago, and comparing them to the speed of all transport we are used to today, I wonder if people will believe what I have written. Yet in the late 1920s such delays were not unusual, the only unusual thing about our delay with the little *Lily* was the reason for it. We could have been held up at Posset with fog followed by a contrary wind, or gale, for a longer period, and other vessels with us without comment from anybody.

We loaded our little vessel that same afternoon; although she carried only 60 tons she needed much more trimming than a trow, for the *Lily* had very small hatchways, safe hatchways enabling her to trade, if necessary anywhere coastwise. Whereas a trow, if not quite open over her cargo space, had very large hatchways and such vessels were mainly confined to trading in the upper Bristol Channel. Those vessels needed very little trimming.

We left Lydney the next day about noon. The wind was from the west, and fresh; this meant that when the strong ebb came down we should have a strong head wind. But this bothered us not at all. Far better to have a head wind than a light fair wind. Loaded, the lovely *Lily* handled like a heavy yacht. In the narrow fairways from Berkeley Pill to the Lyde Rock we tacked repeatedly – probably many more times than were necessary – for the sandbanks beside the fairway can alter their depth by many feet in accordance with the way and strength of the wind, and for this reason we let prudence prevail.

Once past the Lyde we could 'breathe again' for here the waters were wider and deeper; time to put the kettle on in preparation for a belated dinner at Posset. Coming down to Charston we put the little ship on the starboard tack and, with the westerly wind a little forward of the beam, the swiftly flowing current giving more power to the wind, we swept through the Shoots our speed over the ground probably over 11 knots. We were exultant. We had beaten to windward with a loaded vessel down the Severn and through the Shoots. Even in those early days the few masters that sailed their vessels down the Severn were elderly men. The trows were

disappearing and, as the towage was only £1.00, nearly all Appledore sailing vessels would take the tug to Posset. Jack Cornish and
I, in our twenties, were looked on as 'boys'. Had we towed down
the Severn the towages would have amounted to more than a
quarter of our joint share of the freight, such was the penalty of
being in a small vessel.

Soon we were at anchor in Posset pool, no point in going farther
so near to low water. Our appetites had returned. We had a good
meal, scrubbed out the cabin, had a good wash and by then it was
low water. As soon as our little vessel swung upstream from her
anchor we turned into our bunks and a glorious five hours sleep.

Up and about we had the mainsail and mizzen set by 11 and,
with the anchor chain hove in short, we waited for the tide to ease,
drinking tea meantime. At high water we broke out the anchor but
stopped heaving in the chain when the anchor was still below the
forefoot. This was to ensure all the blue clay which we knew would
be clogged between the links a couple of fathom above the anchor
would be washed off before the chain passed through the hawse
pipe. This saved us the labour of drawing many buckets of water
to wash the chain as it came aboard in the darkness.

I quickly set two jibs while the skipper put up the navigation
lights and hauled down the anchor light from the forestay. He then
ran back to the helm leaving me to set the staysail – all done in a
very few minutes. The wind still from the west – a head wind – we
stood out clear of the traffic always to be found thereabout at high
water. Time now for me to heave the rest of the anchor chain in.

The tide sweeping us towards home with only a few tacks and
we were off Clevedon pier. One more short leg off towards the
Clevedon Flats buoy on the port tack, we came about knowing we
could now fetch in below the Blackstone Rock and creep in behind
the tail of the Langford Grounds, and in between those sands and
the Clevedon and Kingston mud flats we should be in the 'gut' (as
we termed it) where as a 15-year-old boy I started fishing for
shrimps.

It was now overcast and very dark and, coming in on that last
tack nothing could be seen of the Somerset shore for the sea banks
obscure all lights from seaward. But we had a good guide; by
keeping the red light on the end of Clevedon pier 'two hands'
(breadths) open from the seaward end of Wain's Hill, that was the
centre of the gut. As soon as the hill obscured the red light we
knew we were near the edge of the mud flats. Making very short
tacks, which was quite easy in our pretty little *Lily*, and watching
our friendly light astern, we soon covered the couple of miles

which put us well below the mouth of the River Yeo and let go
our anchor to the eastward of St Thomas's Head. It was necessary
to get below the river's mouth for should the wind back southerly
or come right off shore the flood tide would always enable us to
get into the mouth of the river.

Crews in those old vessels were forever pitting their wits against
the wind and tides. Four or five hours in our bunks and we had to
be about again, for the flood tide was again obeying the pull of the
moon and racing in around St Thomas's Head, thrusting and prob-
ing its way up through the 'gut' and into the mouth of our old
River Yeo. The wind was still from the west. With plenty of time
the mizzen and two jibs were sufficient to follow the rising tide
into the river. Farther up some of the reaches would bring the wind
nearly ahead, and this would mean dredging part of the way with
our anchor acting as a brake thus giving her steerage way stern
first. Actually, three cable lengths from the pier we had to stow
the sails and drop up stern first with the anchor on the bottom.

Just after we had tied up to the pier and taken of the hatchcloths
and hatches ready for discharging the next day, the afternoon train
from Clevedon to Weston came thundering over the bridge that
carried the track over the river, the driver blowing prolonged blasts
on the whistle as they usually did to welcome a vessel, but this
time we had a feeling it was a derisive whistle because we had been
so long away!!! This was our twelfth day away and, quite without
reason, we felt guilty.

The next morning by the first train down from Clevedon the
crane driver appeared. He also brought with him a tipper to tip the
steel bucket as the crane swung it gyrating over the railway truck.
That tipper had an unenviable job as I have indicated in a previous
chapter. This tipper was needed because, being only the two of us
in the vessel, we had to pay the necessary third hand to tip for us
– the skipper and I had to shovel out the cargo. Shovelling out the
coal was no hardship to us, the 60 tons of coal was transferred to
the trucks in about six hours.

If the details of the work in that unspectacular trip in the *Lily* to
Lydney and back proves to be tedious to read, I excuse myself
because my object is to point out all the changed conditions that
prevail today, 50 years later.

Our share of the Lydney freight was three pounds ten shillings.
Owing to our indisposition we had been 13 days on the trip –
but fog or wind could equally well have hindered us. However,
there were no harbour dues in the isolated River Yeo, and we

had saved a pound on towage down the Severn, and the Lydney dock dues were not heavy. The third share for the ship therefore gave us a balance in hand, even after paying the tipper five shillings for tipping the 60 tons of coal. Five shillings was over the rate. The saving of the £1.00 towage not only expanded our ego but also gave us a balance in hand.

Today, 20th February 1979, I purchased six Jaffa oranges in Weston-super-Mare for about twelve shillings. One wonders what the towage down the Severn would be today. Such is progress. But the pound in the 1920s was worth a golden sovereign.

In a subsequent trip to Lydney for coal for the Railway, we had made an uneventful passage up the Severn with the wind east of south. We had not been to Lydney for quite a few weeks and the tides were cutting, *i.e.*, the highest tide had passed some days before. Coming up to Berkeley Pill, even though it was nearing high water, the tide, as usual, was still running strong. We delayed crossing over toward Lydney as long as was prudent, fearing we may be swept above the pier, a situation always to be avoided by a sailing vessel. Easing off the sheets, for the course across gave us a fair wind and, with a speed of about four knots, we headed for the Lydney pier, but still with the vessel's head down somewhat to allow for the upsweep of the tide. With the skipper at the wheel, I busied myself taking the coiled halyards off the pins, and laying them on the deck ready for running the sails down quickly as we sailed in past the pierhead. About three cables length from the pier I prepared to lower the anchor down to the forefoot for fear our bow should foul anything and damage our planking – all the usual chores one had to do. Slacking away the heavy anchor chain with the anchor hanging usually sends a tremor through a vessel, especially a light vessel, so I did not feel our little ship touch the sand. When the skipper shouted 'We're aground' I thought he was joking until I saw his look of consternation. We were no lower down than we had been many times before, yet with all our care and attention we were trapped. We were well aware, too late, of the reason for our predicament: south west winds strong and persistent helped by fierce tides had piled some of the Lydney sands over the Sanigar sands raising the level three feet or more – we had been away too long and had seen no one to warn us. To avoid one hazard (of being swept up too high) we had encountered another. Such is the River Severn. Had we traded to Lydney more often we should have observed the changed levels of the sands at low water. Touching the ground as we did a few minutes before high water, there was no question of running out a kedge to try to haul her off and with the tides cutting as they were it meant it would be over a week before we floated off again.

Despondent and humiliated we ran down the sails and tied them up. As soon as the water left us high and dry we put a ladder over and walked over the sand to the pier. The contours of the sand around our little vessel were such that had we been 20 feet farther up we should have had plenty of water, we were aground on a ridge only a little wider than our vessel was long.

On the pier the lock gatemen told us they 'had hollered' to try to warn us; but we were nearly three cables to windward of them, and the 'chatter' of the tide around our little ship had drowned their shouts.

Of course our owners were waiting for their coal. Tomorrow they would be ringing the Harbour Office with the usual 'had the *Lily* sailed?' We knew that whoever answered the call would put a good case for us.

Jack Cornish wrote a letter to the manager at Clevedon explaining the incident. He in turn would report it to London. We were not lazy men; before the tides failed to reach us we scrubbed the little vessel's bottom as far as we were able and, having dry weather, we tarred her where we had scrubbed her. Then the white and mast colour paint inside the bulwarks we washed down with soft soap. We felt the *Lily* had never looked better.

The morning we floated off, the wind was east and within about 10 minutes we were in the Lydney Dock. We left the next day, still with a fresh east wind. This gave us an easy passage to Portishead, the booms over the starboard rail most of the way – again we had saved a pound in towage (more than a week's work in pay for one of my father's masons).

Safely back beside the pier in the River Yeo the crane driver, arriving on the first convenient train from Clevedon brought a letter from the London office for the skipper. It was not a nice letter. It was a terrible letter from that faceless man in London no one had ever seen in Clevedon. In acknowledging the report of the grounding of the *Lily* he said, he had 'never heard such rubbish! Was he expected to believe that the bottom of the sea had changed a few yards from the pier and so prevented the *Lily* from entering to dock? Such excuses', he said, 'were unconvincing. It was bad navigation. Nothing else and you are discharged sir, discharged forthwith!!'

Jack and I looked at each other. We should be sorry to leave the *Lily* but we were both single men (actually married men could not afford to be in the *Lily* with such a small cargo). Some vessel would soon be after one or both of us, for our grounding in the Severn was nothing to be ashamed of with those that understood. In any case work was always available for me on the sea walls. Yet 'to have the sack' seemed to us to be a loss of face. However, we had yet to get the coal out to be able to collect our share of the miserable freight.

At the Clevedon office the local manager was somewhat put out by the sacking of the skipper:

'Where am I to get another master?' he said.

Jack (the skipper) told him: 'Why not ask Ted?' (this was myself). 'He knows the river better than I do.' And as he said it he kept nudging me to speak up and agree.

I agreed to give it a trial. The manager, glad of the solution, said he would write to London to say he had found a replacement for Jack, and that was the end of the matter. Going back in the train Jack was jubilant. I felt he was more than glad to be free of the worry and still in the *Lily*.

'Ted,' he said, 'can I still keep the starboard bunk?' (skippers usually sleep on the starboard side of a ship you see).

When I readily agreed he replied, 'But I tell you what, you can have my peaked cap!!!'

Jack always wore a nautical cap.

Back on board Jack signed us both off, and I signed us both on again in our different standings.

A few days later we sailed over to Newport River to load another cargo at the tips. Whilst tying up to the jetty to await our turn under the shute, the tippers came along (obviously expecting to see a new skipper – such was the speed of 'news' in the vessels).

'Hullo skipper,' they said, 'didn't expect to see you here!'

'Why not?', said Jack, looking surprised.

'Three or four vessels have been here and loaded', they said, 'and they all told the same tale!'

'Well,' said Jack, 'you can see I'm still here so it can't be true, can it now?'

Jack was still wearing his peaked cap; it proved to be too small for me. Possibly my head had swelled! As the trade for the little sailing vessels became worse between the wars, cargoes for the *Lily* became few and far between. Even for us two single men the weekly average wages were too small. Sadly we left her laid up in the River Yeo.

Working the ketch Sarah by the shares

Embarrassed by our insolvency Jack and I went our different ways. It was winter with very wet and tempestuous weather – no quick money on the sea walls with my father's men. I made for Avonmouth (for I had a deep-water discharge book) and the very next day shipped as A.B. in an oil tanker, the *British Marshall*. Even in those days that ship was not classed as a big vessel, her carrying capacity being only about six thousand tons. I soon found out why I got the job so easily! The *British Marshall* was a hometrade distributing tanker; she would always load at Swansea, the port where a lot of the tankers discharged their cargoes from Abadan. Never would we take a full cargo anywhere. Usually it was three "drops", such as Foynes, Ipswich and Hull; one favourite call was a port in north Denmark. Our pay was £9,00 per month (30 days). The articles we signed stated that any time worked over 12 hours a day (three 4-hour watches) would be treated as overtime; providing it was not on the days of *arrival* and *sailing*; on those two days no overtime could be claimed before 16 hours had been worked.

Therefore there were very few days when we did not either *arrive* or *sail*. The ship could leave a port at 2 am on, say, a Friday, and arrive at the first call on Saturday ten minutes before midnight, and for those two days the owners could claim 32 hours work of each man before overtime started. Added to that, the massive hawsers necessary to moor a ship of that size, especially in tidal waters, made the work aboard a series of back-breaking exercises, because every time we left a port all ropes had to be stowed below decks, and got up again as we arrived, often the same day. Our worst passage that winter was around the north of Denmark to the Skagerrak and back to Falkirk. The wheel was on an open bridge, the only shelter for the officer of the watch a small covered area in each wing of the bridge, open at the side.

There was an arrangement when one signed on a deep-water ship (I suppose it is the same today) whereby a crew member could draw half a month's pay in advance. This was done by the issue of a payslip, called an advance note, for the benefit of the man's dependent. The note could only be cashed three days after the ship had sailed. Therefore, should the crewman fail to sail in the vessel the owners were safeguarded – the note would not be cashed. However, for those without dependents, like myself, but who wanted money to spend before the ship sailed, there were always enterprising gentlemen ready to change those advance notes into cash – for a price! Of course, if one of the customers failed to sail with the ship, the pimp (for that is what he was) would lose his money. But as the ship owners held the crew members' discharge book, which would be lost should he not honour his agreement, the risk was very slight.

Those swarthy 'benevolent' men were waiting on the steps of the shipping office the day we signed on. I was accosted by a beaming face declaring 'it' had the cheapest store in the district. 'Beaming Face' said he would pay me £3.10s. for my advance note (worth £4.10s.), warning me that if 'any other bums offered me more, it may well be counterfeit money!' I sold him the advance note. He was probably no worse than the others.

I often wonder how, 50 years after my days in the *British Marshall*, the tanks of the tankers are now cleaned. The interior of an oil tanker is made up of a series of tanks, thus breaking up the 'hold' and controlling the movement of the oil as the vessel rolls. The tanks in the *British Marshall* were probably 40 feet or more deep. They were braced both ways inside with heavy section angle iron. There were always some tanks ready to be cleaned, and this was one of the most unpleasant and unseamanlike jobs anyone could be called upon to do.

After the tanks were emptied huge 'windsails' were hoisted over the open lid; the windsails actually hung down some few feet inside the tank. The windsails were round and about three feet in diameter with fin like triangular canvas projections which were supposed to force the wind down inside the windsails and into the tank and force the poisonous gases out. There may have been benzine in the tank, or naphtha or just petrol. A 'cluster' of electric light (maybe 12) bulbs were set up over the tank top, but all the poor 'cleaner' could see as he looked down into the seemingly bottomless pit was a fog of fumes swirling about often, in light winds, too heavy for the wind from the sail to drive it upward out of the tank. On those occasions we waited. The unfortunate seamen whose turn it was to be a 'cleaner' had to don a helmet similar (but less elaborate) to a diver's headgear; there was a pipe leading into the back of the helmet and an adjustable valve in the crown. There was of course a glass front to the helmet. A leather 'skirting' was attached to the base of the helmet forming a cape that covered part of the shoulders and the upper part of the chest and back. This fitted under one's clothing and so made the helmet gas proof – always assuming the helmet was kept supplied with air!

The air pump was similar to the foot pump of a motor car and was worked by the man on deck using his foot whilst he leaned over the rim of the tank watching what went on below – for he also had to haul up the wooden bucket with the sludge that had been shovelled up by the 'cleaner' using a copper hand shovel. The 'cleaner' also carried in his belt a copper-headed hammer; he used this to tap off any large scales of rust that the action of the potent liquids caused to lift off – this was also brought up by the bucket. The perpendicular iron ladder by which one reached the bottom of the tank was welded to the angle iron cross braces. Each bucketful of sludge had to be brought back to the base of the ladder and this, in some cases, meant bending low and some times nearly crawling below the angle braces to keep a straight lead for the line on the bucket otherwise it could not be hauled up. The 'cleaner' also had to be careful of the air pipe which he had to keep hold of and drag it behind him during his gymnastic performances with the bucket, the shovel and the hammer. One of the deck officers would pop down occasionally – without a helmet – glance around and quickly 'be away back up'!

I believe the real object of the cleaning exercise was to get rid of the few gallons of water caused by condensation – the sludge was really oily water. I feel sure that if such conditions prevailed today, no crews would be found for the oil tankers. No wonder I pined for the friendly and familiar atmosphere of the little sailing vessels, the squealing of the blocks as the sails went aloft, the clanking of the windlass as the chain was hove in by manpower – a different world.

It must have been after I had left the *British Marshall* that I was asked to join the ketch *Sarah* (mentioned earlier in this book), a flush-decked trow owned by the Weston, Clevedon and Portishead Light Railway Company. The management had found a new skipper for her; his name was Russel.

Capt Russel came to see me. He was a coasting man and had

been mate of the three-masted schooner *Windermere* for a number
of years. This meant he had been paid by the month. He had never
sailed in a vessel by the share system, as many of the little vessels
then struggling to survive had to do.

He asked if I would join the *Sarah* as mate if only for a time
until he had acquired some local knowledge. I told him I would go
with him for a while for a half share of the crews' share of the
freight. 'But what about the share for the third person?' he said.
I pointed out that if a third hand had to be paid the job would be
no good to either of us.

Years before, when the *Sarah* first came to the River Yeo, she
had just had a Kelvin engine installed, she was therefore classed as
a motor vessel; but I knew the engine had not worked for quite a
time and that it was actually a 'write off'. I gathered it was the
description *M.V. Sarah* in the Railway Company's letter to Bill
Russel that had attracted him to the berth, and was the main reason
for his leaving the lovely *Windermere*. It became clear that he felt
a motor vessel was a 'step up', and an opportunity to pop from
port to port and, at last, earn a living wage!

I had to disillusion him: there was no alternative. For myself,
forever hankering after the sailing vessels, it was another Heaven-
sent opportunity to sail again in and out of our local river, the west
boundary of the isolated village I loved.

I have already related the hard times we experienced in the little
ketch *Lily* belonging to the same Railway Company, but the *Lily*
carried only 60 tons. Without being too optimistic I thought the
Sarah, with a carrying capacity of double the amount of cargo,
might give us a reasonable return for our labours – providing her
owners managed her in a proper manner. They were not really
nautical minded, you see.

We left the river one fine morning with a southerly wind and
ran across the ebb and anchored in the mouth of the Usk. On the
flood we sailed up to the jetties, for the wind was still favourable,
and loaded our coal the next morning. We found the gear in the
Sarah quite heavy enough for two men to handle. Her main boom
was about 30 feet long and at least nine inches in diameter. The
main gaff also 30 feet long tapering from eight inches at the throat
to six inches at the peak. The mainsail, probably 120 square yards
of heavy canvas attached to the heavy gaff – especially in wet
weather – even by using the dolly winch, was too much for two
men to hoist aloft and set up quickly; it was a slow and arduous
exercise. Four hands would have been about right.

The freight for the 120 tons of coal from Newport to the River

Yeo and discharged would amount to about £12.10s and the share
of this for the crew would be £4.3s.4d or a little over £2 for each
of us. There was no alternative there than to work the vessel
short-handed. However hard this may sound, we were not un-
happy men, for we were free. After my winter in the *British
Marshall*, where the bunks in the forecastle were in tiers, and where
the deck head and sides were for ever sweating out condensation,
and the steam 'heating' pipes the coldest metal of all, where too,
Englishmen were in the minority. After that degrading kind of
seafaring, the homely labours in the *Sarah*, and my sense of inde-
pendence were like a harvest of joy.

Although we had dropped down the River Usk overnight, we
could not leave until high water on the next tide because of a fresh
wind from the west. But as soon as the ebb came down we set all
sail except the topsail and, on the starboard tack, the wind holding
us up against the ebb in a couple of hours we were skirting the tail
of the Langford grounds, the west wind strong enough to dispel
all fear of the little race there always was around St Thomas's Head.

What a contrast the cumbersome old *Sarah* was to the ketch
Lily! The latter always quick to respond never seemed to stop
sailing in stays even on the shortest of tacks. The *Sarah*, twice her
size, seemed to lumber along, smashing her big bluff bow into the
headsea, seemingly to scatter it in a smother of white water on
either side, an exciting picture to watch if one did not mind getting
wet.

The skipper, unused to trows, was intrigued by the wake astern.
The heavy rudder, hung as it was like a mighty door (6 in. thick)
on the transom and so close to the surface of the water, as it
responded to the action of the wheel caused much commotion in
the already boiling wake. The ship seemed to be dragging the sea
along. Yet with it all the *Sarah* was, in spite of the noise and the
flying water, buoyant enough, her bulwarks were high, she seemed
powerful and we were well pleased.

Inside St Thomas's Head we rounded to and let go the anchor.
Here we were about a half a mile below the mouth of our River
Yeo, and sheltered by Woodspring Hill from any westerly wind.
A mile and a half up the Somerset coast we could see the upper
storey of my home – built in the 17th century as a watchhouse.

Our quarters in the *Sarah* were in the forecastle – not unusual
when an engine was installed in the cabin aft. We never saw that
engine running; my information concerning its 'demise' had proved
to be correct. The quarters were roomy and comfortable; far better
than they could have been before the engine was installed. We ate,

and slept well for about four hours that day in the lee of Woodspring, and on the early flood with the wind just west of south and
not much of it, we edged slowly up towards the river's mouth. My
object was (for I was the 'pilot') to let Capt Russel see as much as
possible of the river before the tide covered too much of its outline.
This meant the vessel would not have water over the bar, but with
the wind as it was the water was smooth, so that when we touched
the ground the mud there was very soft, the ship would come to
no harm.

We did not even feel the vessel touch the soft ground of the bar
for the wind had become lighter. The skipper went aloft, for this
gave him a good opportunity to take stock of landmarks that might
serve him in good stead when, or if, he should arrive off the mouth
of the river when a high spring tide might be covering even the
saltings.

Floating off the bar, and with hardly enough wind to give us
steerage way, when we were well into the river we lowered the
sails, stuck the old ship's bow into the bank and, as her stern swung
up stream with the tide, let go the anchor with just enough chain
out to allow her to drop slowly astern, slower than the current,
thus ensuring the rudder had enough purchase to keep the vessel's
head in midstream. This was the only way (the usual way) to cover
the last mile up river to the pier when the vessel had no wind. It
was a simple method to use the current when there was no wind.
A method used by Captain Cook in the *Endeavour* and, no doubt,
a century before that.

We covered that mile stern first in less than an hour and were
tied up long before high water. Thus ended the first trip in the
Sarah – except of course we had to shovel out the 120 tons of coal
before we could claim our share of about £2 each of the total
freight.

Two or three trips later we arrived off the mouth of the river
less than an hour before high water. It was an evening tide, which
meant it was a spring tide in that part of the channel, with the wind
again about south west. No need to worry about water over the
bar that evening, there was plenty of water everywhere, too much
really because on entering the river itself we found the tide in some
places completely covering the saltings. This was really a hazard
for one had to guess the centre of the river without any guide from
the saltings. However, we had a good breeze and though it would
mean pinching the old ship up in what we called Pugs Pit reach,
with the topsail set, we foresaw no difficulty. About three cable
lengths below the pier we had to luff up pretty close to the wind

but only for a distance of about six lengths of the ship. But as soon as the luffs of the sails started to lift the old *Sarah* seemed to lose way in the most unexpected manner. It was still half an hour to high water so that our speed, plus the flowing tide, should have taken us through the short reach with no bother. I quickly called to Bill Russel (for I was at the helm) to let go the anchor, and this was speedily done, but before the anchor had a lead the vessel fell away to leeward and we touched the bank. Too late we realised the reason for our misfortune. Recent heavy rains had swollen the rivers inside the sea banks, and those streams, discharging the flood waters into the upper Yeo, had piled up and penned the tidal stream bringing it to a halt before the natural high water.

The *Sarah*'s loaded draught was between nine and ten feet; sounding around with a long boathook we found we were aground on a sunken part of the saltings (i.e., a salty marsh that grows a rye grass), in other words we were aground on a landslide, about a quarter of an acre in extent. This was a disaster, because the highest of the spring tides had gone. We should be lucky if we floated off on the next high water and this meant we should be neaped for about ten days within sight of the railway pier! Imagine our feelings and *mine* in particular. Besides, from the deck we could look down over the green fields of my native village. Our masts and rigging would attract every eye in the village for every hour of the day. The loss of face! My cup of humiliation was full.

Down below, over the inevitable cup of tea, we looked at each other across the table, wondering what sort of defence we could put forward for the faceless man in London. The top management was so appallingly ignorant of the unavoidable things that could happen to ships and crews in their never-ending efforts to use and battle with the elements; we knew that reason would never prevail. I was glad to realise that Bill Russel had no thought of blame to myself. I thought of my father at home a little less than a mile away, for he would have quickly realised we were ashore at high water.

However, it was time for supper. The tide had left us; we stoked the fire and lit the gimbaled lamp. Suddenly we felt the ship shudder, our stomachs seemed to rise within us, we heard a dreadful roar of water – a kind of 'swalloping' sound (a Somerset term), then the rattle of the anchor chain around the windlass. We fell over each other – two frightened men scrabbling to reach the deck! But it wasn't an earthquake; we were amazed – the *Sarah* was afloat nearly in the middle of the river, a huge island of mud and slurry along her starboard side.

When the ship fell away to leeward and grounded on the saltings, evidently the bank had been steep-to undercut by the current around the bend of the river. After the tide had left us, the *Sarah*, having 120 tons of coal in her hold and this, added to the weight of the ship, I suppose another 100 tons – had been too much for the bank to support. Fortunately there was still plenty of water in the river and this, with the added 'cushion' of the mud outside and beneath her, allowed the ship to come to no harm. We were out of trouble, but greatest of all was the relief for the saving of face!! Immediately there was enough water in the river to swing the little ship the next morning, we dropped her astern under her anchor and were safely tied up to the pier before the first train came down from Clevedon.

Later a local 'official' arrived with the crane driver.

'You fellows haven't been long away,' said the official. 'Did you manage to start the engine?'

'Engine!' said Bill Russel, with a look of disgust. 'We sailed her up here last night or nearly so. We anchored a little way below in Pugs Pit reach!!'

Which was perfectly true, of course.

What about the island of mud and earth in the middle of the river? Well, immediately the tide had ebbed out of the Yeo there was still the torrent of flood water six feet deep boiling past our little vessel in the centre of the river, before the next flood came this quickly eroded the 'island of mud' and swept it away. But the roar of the water kept us awake; this did not matter, we had arrived with another cargo, only now to shovel out the 120 tons of coal, draw our wages of a bit over £4 and share it between us!

One vessel that gives me a lot of pleasure to recall, and brings me a most pleasurable mental picture of how she looked as I knew her in the late 1920s, is the Bridgwater ketch *Annie Christian*. Yet such are the complexities of the human mind, she is the one vessel I actually sailed in where I am unable to recall the details of the trading we managed to do in her, with the exception of one cargo. That cargo was pit props from Watchet in Somerset to Newport in the Bristol Channel. The reason of my confusion of thought may be because I joined her three or four times, and each time after a couple of cargoes the little ship was laid up, no cargoes being offered by the ship brokers – except for freights no one wanted.

My first sight of the *Annie Christian* was at Lydney (said to be the smallest port in England) when I was a lad in the little ketch-rigged decked trow the *Jane*. The *Annie Christian* was lying in the canal, her reflection mirrored in the still water on a summer's day.

In addition to her bowsprit she had a very long and graceful jib
boom, and both spars were newly varnished. The *Jane's* bowsprit
was painted with what we called 'mast colour' paint, and trowlike,
her bowsprit reached out nearly level over the water, whereas the
jib boom of the *Annie Christian* seemed to rear up pointing sky-
ward, the guys and bobstay painted white. The ship herself beside
the rather boxlike *Jane* looked to me a mighty beautiful thing, all
curves and graceful sweeps, her tail masts and spars scraped and
oiled, bringing out the lovely grain of the pitchpine. Then again
her decks were outstandingly white, laid with the narrow planking
following the curves of the ship. Everything was bright and smart.
I believe she was coasting then, her crew paid by the month.
Whoever owned her at that time saw to it she was well found and
smartly maintained.

Many years after that first encounter I was asked to join her as
mate, she was lying in the docks at Bridgwater and was owned by
the Somerset Trading Company. Her skipper was Jack Cornish
who, as I have stated, was at one time captain of the ketch *Lily*.
The *Annie Christian* had not changed much over the years; she was
still very smart and tidy, purely a sailing vessel with her elegant jib
boom which I found just as fascinating as I did when I first saw
her.

The *Annie Christian* was one of the few 'vessels' with the outside
of the bulwarks painted other than black. Hers were painted naval
grey. This added to her smartness, but one drawback to it was the
necessity to paint them more often. It was the first job I noticed
needed doing the first day I joined her. The owners never quibbled
about a gallon or two or paint, so the bulwarks were scrubbed and
repainted before we sailed from Bridgwater; this included the gam-
mon knee which, being a continuation of the stem as it were, was
painted black. The fiddle head and other carvings were picked out
in 'gold' colour paint. This beneath the varnish bowsprit looked
most effective against the background of the grey bulwarks. Each
time I was in the *Annie Christian* we found it necessary to repaint
those bulwarks, for ships laid up became shabby far more quickly
than ships at work, and grey is quick to show it.

Jack Cornish and I, with another Weston man, worked her
three-handed. We would have liked to stay in her, but the slump
had by then become more acute; the cargoes for vessels without
auxiliary engines just weren't about. When we went to Watchet to
load the pit props for the Welsh mines the Harbour Master was
Capt Redd. Before he became Harbour Master he was master of
the Watchet-owned schooner, the *Naiad*. I recall he was a kind

man, he gave us some very sound advice. Most welcome of all was his praise of the appearance of our little ship.

The pit props we loaded came from the woods, on the nearby Quantock Hills. The timber was larch, or fir, in lengths of about six feet, the diameter from four to eight inches. We, the crew, had to help stow the cargo. Each of us was provided with a short hook with a 'tee' handle; the curve of the hook ended in a very wicked looking spike. Most of the log handling was done with the hooks. The hobblers, used to that tool, could land a log almost anywhere by 'shooting' them in any direction by a snatch of the hook; we, the crew, were apt to drive the point of the hook in too deeply, we could not 'release' it in time and so sometimes followed the log. Of course we had a deck cargo, but even then we were not loaded down to the Plimsoll line. I forget the freightage, but I know it was a very meagre return.

The last time we left the *Annie Christian* – owing to there being no cargoes available, she had to lay up again in Bridgwater – although I recall we discharged a cargo of coal from her, I cannot remember what port we brought it from; it was probably Lydney. What I do remember is the footmarks on the sheets (floor) of the forecastle discovered just before we were due to leave to catch the evening train to Weston-super-Mare. We had been down the cabin aft having a yarn and settling up our shares of the freight with the master, Jack Cornish. We had never left the *Annie Christian* other than clean, not altogether because we liked her clean to come back to, but it was the usual thing for a decent crew to do. Anxious as the three of us were to catch the train, the footprints worried me. Jack Cornish and the third hand thought it was nothing to worry about – 'anybody could see the floor had been scrubbed', they said. But despite their protests I decided to miss the train. When I left, the forecastle sheets were again snow white, but I had missed the rail connection from Yatton to Clevedon and so had to walk the four miles to my home at Kingston Seymour. After shovelling out the cargo of coal that same day, the four mile walk after midnight left me footsore and weary, yet satisfied and happy with what I had done. It may appear that I had been too finical; yet such was the training I had received in my early days in the *Jane* of the importance of cleanliness and tidiness, I could never after find peace of mind in a slovenly ship. I refer of course to Capt Leonard Smart, who was part-owner and master of the trow *Jane*. Capt Andrew Murdock in my second ship the *Garlandstone* was nearly as particular. I have always been thankful to those two seamen for their example.

Contrary to what we expected we never went back to the *Annie Christian*. The next time I saw that – *to me* – very beautiful vessel was in (I believe) the year 1943, in the Lydney Canal. She was lying beside the bank loaded with coal. I did not at first recognise her, yet felt I must know her, but her name was the *Ade* and I had never heard of the *Ade* before. Here was a vessel with a shortened topmast, a peg bowsprit, and a motor winch adjacent to the mainmast. She obviously had a motor auxiliary.

I soon discovered she was the old *Annie Christian* – but what a transformation! Gone was her beautiful jib boom. The once bright pitchpine masts and spars were then black with grime, the bulwarks no longer grey. Her decks, once white, were now the same colour as the seams between the planks; oil and coal dust had joined forces to obliterate every bit of white planking that had so long prevailed. I felt she was a ship in mourning for the beautiful vessel she once was! Even her name was cut down to just a miserable three letters! I turned away sad at heart, thinking of the night I had stayed behind to scrub the already clean forecastle sheets, and wondered what those sheets now looked like down below those blackened decks.

The three-masted schooner Mary Jones

I have recently read an article in a Sunday newspaper written by Mr Frank Driscoll which leads me to think of the three-masted schooner *Mary Jones*. The first time I saw the three-masted schooner *Mary Jones* was when I was in the ketch *Garlandstone*, and we were on passage to Waterford with a cargo of salt. That first sight of her is easy to recall because it was such an outstandingly beautiful sunrise. We had cleared the Smalls lighthouse just as dawn was breaking one very bright and clear autumn morning. Soon the seemingly almost horizontal rays of the sun lit up the crests of the moderate seas, occasioned by a fresh east wind, setting the sea on fire with a multitude of colours wonderful to see, a morning of magic. Away to the westward some five or six miles, we could see a three-masted schooner. Her sails, some tanned, some white, stood out in sharp relief. She was on the port tack and rapidly reducing the distance between us – she was obviously using an auxiliary engine. The *Garlandstone*, using only her sails, was making about four knots. Capt Murdock, our skipper, coming on deck immediately identified the schooner as the *Mary Jones*. 'Haven't seen her for months; aye, years!' he said. But he knew all about her, telling me she was owned by Capt W Shaw, brother of the owner and master of the schooner *Cambourne*.

Soon we could hear the thump, thump, thump of her semi-diesel engine. She seemed to be storming along, the spray from the moderate billow flying over her foredeck, wetting her headsails as they slanted into the rays of the sun, flashing and sparkling with every roll of the ship. She appeared to be twice the size of the *Garlandstone*, but she did not carry twice her cargo. She was obviously loaded with oats – a common cargo from Ireland – for she was 'light on', her Plimsoll line well out of the water. That lovely morning as she swept past us, not more than a cable's length away, I was struck by her flared bows, more evident owing to the lightness of her cargo, giving her a look of boldness and solidity, and giving myself a feeling of envy, even though I was proud to be in the *Garlandstone*.

Little did I think that within three years I should be asked to join her.

The telegram asking me to join the *Mary Jones* as mate came, I think, in 1928. It was sent by a firm of shipbrokers in Newport and, the fact that it was sent by those shipbrokers points to the fact that I must have just left the ketch *Annie Christian*, otherwise those brokers would not have sent the wire, for that same firm did all the business of the *Annie Christian*. The *Mary Jones* was lying beside the coal tips in the River Usk, loaded with coal for (if I recall rightly) New Ross in Ireland. When I arrived at Newport I found that Capt Shaw lived there, so that the first time I met him (and his wife) was at his home. He was however born at Connah's Quay where his family belonged.

After climbing down the well-known perpendicular ladder attached to the slimy piles of the tall jetties in the Newport River, and making myself known to the crew – this was done by walking forward and calling down the scuttle (it was now dark) and seeing three pairs of eyes – Irish eyes! – looking up at me but unable to clearly see me wondering, no doubt, 'What kind of fellow could this be without an Irish accent!' I went down and let them know the worst! My accent told them I was from Appledore and they, not knowing a Somerset accent from a Devonshire one, I did not disillusion them! Appledore men are mainly good men.

The cabin of the *Mary Jones* as far as I could see had not been altered much to accommodate the engine, the space apparently being taken from the hold: the mate's room on the port side of the cabin had not been interferred with. The auxiliary engine was a 60 h.p. Bolinder with two cylinders. The head of each cylinder contained a bulb about four inches in diameter. These had to be heated by an enormous blow lamp with two burners fixed in position to heat the bulbs to start the engine. When the engine was running these bulbs kept themselves hot enough to fire the gases in the cylinders and this, I understood, was termed semi-diesel. To start the engine it was necessary to heat the bulbs to *orange* colour. Should they become red hot the engine would backfire or even go the opposite to clockwise – as it ought to go.

If you were lucky and the Bolinder started first time, a pump could be put into operation and the engine would replenish the

compressed air in the air cylinder. Compressed air was necessary
to start the engine; no manpower could swing it. Should the Bolinder fail to start in the first two attempts we then held our breath
in fear and trembling!! For there was now only one chance, for
should it fail for the third time – which it did on a few occasions
– the air cylinder, about six or seven feet long, had to be pumped
up by foot pump and this could be three hours of very tiring work.
It could be pumped three parts full pretty quickly, but to get it up
to the required pressure (I believe it was eighty pounds) was an
exercise to be dreaded. All hands had to 'have a go', the skipper
'showing the way' because it was his pet. Once started the engine
would seem to go on for ever, thumping day after day without
pause.

Once when leaving Devonport with a cargo of scrap iron from
the naval dockyard the engine failed to start with the first two
attempts. 'All the Navy' seemed to be watching us, for the rail of
a destroyer not many feet away was lined with men. An irate naval
commander kept calling to us to 'come ahead', to get out of the
way of the destroyer. I had all the mooring ropes in except for two
slip ropes that could be 'whipped in', in a few seconds. I went half
way down the ladder to the engine room to see what was happening
just as Capt Shaw pulled the lever that released the air from the air
cylinder. The engine gave a roar, I looked at the fly wheel – it was
going the wrong way, the engine was running anti-clockwise.

'They're playing hell up on the quay,' I shouted.

'Give me a couple of minutes to warm her up a bit,' said the
Captain, 'then I'll put her in reverse and that may take us clear of
the lock.'

With one of the hands on each slip rope, I stood looking down
through the engine room skylight; Capt Shaw gestured to me to
let go the lines. I called to the two sailors to haul in, the Capt
pulled the reverse lever, the old ship started to tremble and then
slowly move ahead! Simultaneously, the irate officer with the gold
rings on his sleeve came storming back along the quay calling, 'Are
you ever coming ahead?' 'Yes,' I said, 'right now. The captain has
put her in reverse!' Thus ended a very stormy ten minutes with the
naval brass. Once clear of the dockyard we quickly set the main
and a couple of jibs, for fortunately the wind was fair; the Captain
stopped the engine, and it was not long before we were clear of
Drake's Island.

We soon had the rest of the sail set and everything coiled away;
time now to start pumping up the air bottle, for once we rounded

Lands End we should have a head wind, and head winds were what engines were made for.

In relating the episode of the Bolder engine I have run ahead of myself. I return to the River Usk and the day of sailing, the day after I joined that fine old vessel.

The *Mary Jones*, like all topsail schooners, had her yards taken down when the auxiliary engine was installed, thus enabling the ship to be worked with less hands. A double topsail schooner could not sail so close to the wind as a ketch or a fore and aft schooner. Furthermore a fore and aft schooner – or a ketch – with a fairly powerful auxiliary running and using her sails at the same time can sail much closer to the wind than a vessel under sail only. There was no point therefore in retaining the double topsails of a schooner if an engine was to be made good use of to make quick passages.

However, Capt Shaw had given his vessel a light squaresail yard – on the foremast of course – I believe it was about 25 feet long, so that whenever the wind was abaft the beam we would set that huge sail and its pulling power added considerably to the speed of the ship.

That first morning as we motored out of the River Usk (Newport River) setting all the sails on the three masts with the aid of the motor winch, for Capt Shaw had quickly let it be known that the winch could be used at all times to save the laborious hauling and swigging up of the heavy sails.

There was also a chain arrangement leading from the winch to the windlass whereby the anchor could be hove up. This attitude of mind was quite contrary to that found in other vessels I had been in, especially as we had three hands in the forecastle.

After the smaller vessels such as the *Garlandstone*, the *Annie Christian* and the bonny little *Lily*, the *Mary Jones*, although she could only carry – if I recall correctly – about 190 tons, was quite a ship. To me on that first day aboard, there seemed to be plenty of room everywhere. According to Capt Shaw she had been built in the 1860s and was in the Newfoundland trade. Her fore deck swept so sharply upwards that one felt one was walking 'uphill', and this, with her breast-high bulwarks flared outwards gave her that bold appearance. There was a half deck forward for spare sails.

It was not difficult to imagine her in the Newfoundland trade during her early days. Well manned and well found, and well able to stand up to anything that came at her during her crossings of the wild and unpredictable North Atlantic.

We experienced fresh north west winds that first morning after we passed the Flatholm on our journey down the Bristol Channel.

It seemed strange to me to hear the rhythmic beat of the Bolinder engine in a vessel at sea with plenty of wind under sail, but with the wind slanting off the coast of Wales there was not much head sea. The *Mary Jones* with her booms aboard very close hauled on the starboard tack, called to mind my first sight of her that beautiful morning in the Irish Sea. But there was no sparkle on the sea on this particular morning, instead we had an ominous lowering sky with the wind increasing.

I quickly became used to the heavy throb of our 'passage making' engine, and the very noticeable tremble it caused throughout the ship. In fact should it stop, or have to be stopped during my watch below and I was asleep, it immediately woke me up.

That night, the north wester persisting, and knowing what the sea would be like when we opened up the 'north channel', (as we called it), Capt Shaw let prudence prevail and we went into that very snug anchorage in Angle Bay in Milford Haven. There we all had a good supper and a quiet night in our bunks. I found I got on very well with Capt Shaw. I thought of the *Garlandstone* and the nights we had dodged off Milford Haven with the staysail to windward, the master disdaining the very thought of Angle Bay! Here indeed was comfort.

Soon after daylight we were awakened by some shouts from a steam trawler; they had just returned from the fishing grounds and had 'crept' right alongside and were hanging on to the forerigging. They were proffering a cane fishing basket over half full of lovely fresh fish including two huge plaice. 'Any chance of a bit of Lydney coal for the galley fire?' said the skipper. We gave them three baskets of coal (although the coal was loaded at Newport!). It was the best house coal and everybody was well satisfied. We were lucky to be lying the farthest off otherwise the fish would have been bartered to some other vessel.

I never heard of a cargo of coal that when discharged weighed out short. There was always plenty for the three fires in most vessels – cabin, forecastle and galley. Having a half deck in the *Mary Jones* there was seldom less than half a ton down there. Evidently the merchants, or the colleries, allowed plenty for waste, such as overspilling from the coal chutes, etc. Any vessel which had not had a cargo of coal for a few weeks, and was low on coal for the fires, would replenish their modest requirements from a vessel that was loaded with coal – or had just discharged a cargo. A vessel was seldom refused, it was the unwritten rule. It may not have been strictly honest, but no one even thought about that. I should have stated above that the coal the trawlers carried in their bunkers was not suitable for domestic fires.

We were not the only vessel windbound in Angle Bay during that north wester. Daybreak showed us four other vessels. One of these, which surprised us, was the trow *Jonadab*. We understood she was bound from Liverpool to London River and had been in Angle a fortnight. She was, of course, a decked trow and except for her huge rudder hanging on the transom – 'out in the wet' as we termed it – she had not the boxlike appearance of the majority of her class, instead she was rounded and shapely and had a sheer. Incidentally, at one time during the last war I was master of the *Jonadab* when she was a barge, a towing barge. She would over-run any tug when she was loaded with the wind aft. On one occasion when bound for Ely Harbour to load coal, in a strong north-east wind she over-ran the tug off Portishead Point – we were just out of Bristol River – and on the back surge the eight inch towrope parted as if it was thread. We drove away to leeward too quickly for the tug to catch us and it was only by letting go the anchor (where I judged there were no rocks) and bringing her into the wind just in time we were saved from disaster. Before low water we grounded on a patch of soft mud in Woodhill Bay.

Another of the four vessels with us that time in Angle was the *Earl Cairns*; built at Connah's Quay about 20 years after the *Mary Jones*, she was launched from the same place.

After two days the weather moderated and all the vessels except the *Jonadab* got under way.

As soon as it was daylight that quiet morning in September, the clank, clank, clank which was the music of the heavy paws as they dropped into the cogs of the windlass barrels, as the four vessels hove in their cables; the sound magnified by the quietness of the morning must have awakened many people on the shore. If it failed to do so, then the fleeting over the chain cables as they overrode the turns of the windlass, and the flaking of the heavy chains along the decks would have denied sleep to all but the very deaf.

The *Mary Jones'* anchor was the first aboard, this was thanks to the 'chain arrangement' and the motor winch and plenty of hands to attend to things. Our fore and aft sails were set before we started to weigh the anchor. Before the anchor was broken out there came a roar from the engine room – the Bolinder had started first time! As soon as the anchor was well clear of the bottom, I signalled to the captain now on deck by the wheel; he put the engine in gear and we were away well ahead of the other vessels with a minimum of labour. I was prejudiced against engines, but I was forced to admit they made life more easy aboard a vessel.

Most, if not all, of the deck work was left to me; the captain's main interest was the engine room. Later he was to prove to be a very competent engineer.

Looking astern we saw the *Earl Cairns*, her topsails aback to pay her head off to fill her other sails, then her headsails went up, her yards were hauled round and she was away; all very smartly done. Could the scene, that lovely morning, have been filmed, such a picture today, especially in colour, would be priceless. An exercise very little different had the same ship, the *Earl Cairns*, being got under way in the days before Trafalgar.

The next morning we were beside the quay in New Ross, having motored with an east wind behind us all the way.

Whilst thinking of Milford Haven, three or four months later in the middle of winter, the *Mary Jones*, bound this time for Rosslare, had occasion through inclement weather to seek shelter in Angle Bay again. By a coincidence our cargo of house coal had again been loaded in Newport River. We had news that on the same tide on which we left Newport the *Cambourne*, a three-masted schooner owned by Hugh Shaw, our skipper's brother, had sailed from Lydney bound for Courtmacsherry. This owing to the tides put her 12 hours behind us.

During supper that night Capt Shaw said, 'Maybe our Hughie will be in here tomorrow, shouldn't think even he will venture farther down this weather.' Hugh Shaw was noted as a 'hard weather man'.

Sure enough, the next morning the *Cambourne* came motoring into the harbour, her red sails reefed down and white with salt. 'Hughie' had evidently been down towards the Smalls and 'opened up the North Channel' and decided the risk of damage to his ship was too great.

As they came to anchor not far from us we launched our boat and Capt Billy Shaw and myself went across to help tie up the *Cambourne*'s sails. We had had a good rest, we knew we should be welcome; friendly crews often helped out in such circumstances. The *Cambourne*'s sails were of the best heavy canvas, and that morning were stiff as boards with brine.

That was my first meeting with Hugh Shaw, quick, lean, and fast talking; I took to him at once. I could see that the crew red eyed and weary as they were, were summing me up, especially Jack Kennedy, the mate. Incidentally, about three years later, Jack, a good and trustworthy seaman and highly thought of by Capt

Hugh, was drowned when he slipped off the stock of the anchor which, I believe, had become foul of the bobstay, and Jack had slid down and was trying to clear it whilst the *Cambourne* was motoring through the shoots in the River Severn. Only Jack's hat was ever found.

That same evening, in the *Cambourne*'s cabin with the two Shaw brothers was the first time I heard a radio, or the wireless as we called it, other than through the medium of the 'cat's whisker'! There the voice came out of a mahogany box which contained the loudspeaker.

Strange as it may seem now nearly 50 years later, to me at the time it appeared fantastic that a voice was there for all to hear without the use of headphones.

Both the Shaws were fond of reading. We had taken half a dozen books across with us in the boat to exchange for some others we hoped to get from the *Cambourne*. Hugh Shaw's rack was full so we were able to take our pick. Immediately we were back in the cabin of the *Mary Jones* we put the books in the oven of the cabin fireplace (that fire was kept burning at all times, except in hot weather, by the cook). We did this as a safeguard against any bugs there may be in the back bindings of the books – a favourite hiding place. This may sound a strange thing to do, nevertheless it was *very necessary*, for in most of the coastal sailing vessels, including also the Severn trows, bugs (bed bugs) would be found. This was certainly not on account of uncleanliness, for family ships with most particular and scrupulously clean crews were seldom free from those unpleasant creatures. Their presence could be explained by the fact that the massive timbers from which the hulls were constructed, covered as they were with the ornamental woodwork of the bunks, cupboards, lockers, and panelling in the living quarters, especially the cabins, made an ideal hiding place. There they could lay their eggs in strongholds that could not be stormed; and the warm and cosy atmosphere of the quarters forming them into ready-made incubators that were never completely free of the vermin. These creatures were never troublesome, or seldom seen, in daylight – or lamplight. But immediately one was in the bunk and turned out the light they would start to bite – usually at the back of the neck.

Sulphur candles would destroy any bugs the fumes could reach but, of course, did not affect the eggs. The procedure was to place three or four candles in bowls in the cabin or the forecastle, or both, light the wicks, dash up the companionway and batten down the hatchway with canvas covers, likewise the skylight and ventilators, and not open anything up for at least 12 hours. It was then some twelve hours before the quarters were tolerable to live in. It was this time factor that made it impossible for a working ship to fumigate more often, such as if the vessel was in her home port, or in a drydock or shipyard for repairs.

A week or ten days after the fumigation other eggs would hatch out and the 'fun' would start all over again. Could another fumigation have been given to kill off the 'new generation' the cure would have been much more lasting. I found it was seldom a bug was taken ashore in anyone's clothing.

However, back to that night in the cabin of the *Mary Jones*, warm and comfortable listening to the wind howling through the rigging, whilst we had our supper, and discussing the radio with the loud speaker. Capt Billy said he would rather not have one aboard, 'Otherwise', he said, 'if one listened to the predictions of the weather those fellows gave us, we'd all be too scared to put to sea!' It was then we suddenly smelt burning. We looked at each other; the Capt said 'Good God, Ted, the books!' I scrabbled to open the oven door, a cloud of smoke billowed out – Hugh Shaw's books were burnt to a cinder!

The next day, although the wind moderated, it was still very blusterly, telling us that the sea outside would still be formidable. However, the *Cambourne* left, her sails reefed, her captain, no doubt, judging the weather would continue to moderate. He was right too. Capt Hughie was restless and a go-getter, whereas his brother was more composed and not quite so ambitious. The *Cambourne* was better found than the *Mary Jones* – she needed to be with the master she had. The gear in the *Mary Jones* was not quite so good.

On one occasion we had taken a cargo of oats from Ireland to Swansea. There we were fortunate to get fixed for a cargo of patent manure for Truro. Before we started to load the cargo for Truro the captain went home to Newport, telling me as soon as the vessel was loaded to take her out to the Fish Quay. The Fish Quay was a timber structure of considerable length outside the dock entrance and on the eastward side and, of course, in tidal water.

I can not recall the name of the dock we loaded in, but I well remember there was a busy traffic-carrying swing bridge that had to be opened to let a vessel reach the entrance.

The morning I had arranged for the bridge to be opened to shift the *Mary Jones* to the Fish Quay came in very windy – but not enough to cancel the arrangement. It was a very worrying time for me on account of the (to me) uncertainty of the old Bolinder

engine. With Capt Shaw aboard to manage the engine the handling
of the ship did not bother me at all. But, as I have already indicated,
the engine was fickle and temperamental and I was no engine man.
That morning the engine started on the third attempt, thus leaving
no air in the bottle to restart her should she stall; and it had been
known on occasion for it to be difficult to knock the engine out of
gear except by stopping it completely, or slowing it down so much
that it would stall. What if this should happen should we have to
wait, and probably go astern, should a traffic jam make it impossible for the bridge to be opened on time? Added to this there was
the strong cross wind sweeping over that long and open dock, and
the *Mary Jones'* three masts and rigging held a lot of wind.

I shall never forget that awful few minutes of worry. I had given
three blasts on the foghorn (I believe it had to be three). I dare not
slow the engine too much lest the wind take charge owing to too
little steerage way: too much traffic about to allow us to up helm
and make a complete circle. I was just about to 'knock the engine
out' of gear, and tell them to stand by the anchor when we saw the
bridge begin to move – we were saved.

I had a lot of that sort of thing in the *Mary Jones*; I did not at
all mind the responsibility except for the unpredictable engine. In
that ship I discovered that to be the mate of such a vessel on passage
at sea, as long as one was a capable seaman, could handle a ship
under sail, and had elementary knowledge of coastal navigation
there was nothing to worry about – one could always call the
captain anyway! It was the shifting around in docks and harbours
when the captain was home, and to be expected to do it with an
engine which, although it would run 'flat out' for days on end,
seemed to object to 'pottering around'.

At one time when motoring up to a berth in Plymouth dock
loaded with oats – with such a light cargo in, and our vessel's high
flared bows it was impossible for the captain to see anything directly ahead from the after deck – I gave the usual signal for Capt
Shaw to put the engine out of gear ready to go into reverse when
necessary. But still the vessel came ahead. I frantically waved for
him to go astern, then I saw he was desperately trying to pull the
lever into reverse! I called to the waiting boys to let go the anchor
for we were almost heading 'stem on' to the quay wall. My heart
was in my mouth and I instantly thought of our figurehead, the
Maud Mary. But no damage came to the ship. There was a train
load of loaded coal trucks stationary on the lines only a few feet
from the edge of the quay. Our bowsprit end, like a mighty ram-
road caught the centre of a 10-ton truck pushing it up and over

nearly on its side, the buffers all the way down the train clanging as they each moved up a few inches, acting like a catapault. The *Mary Jones* was saved. The underside of the bowsprit, about three feet from the stem, only a few inches above the quay; the forehead of the *Maud Mary* only inches from the wall!

Captain Billy, putting a pound note in my hand said 'Go and see the shunter fellow Ted, see what you can do!' I did what I could, for a pound note was almost a week's wages for the railwayman. There was no more bother. Was it any wonder I was apprehensive when I was responsible for handling the ship in confined waters with such an engine?

Back now to the Fish Quay in the entrance to the docks at Swansea. We laid beside that quay for three weeks, for that windy morning was the forerunner of nearly a month's continuous gales. Many ships were lost in the British Channel, one big steamship off Hartland Point. It was in the latter part of the 1920s. During that time Capt Shaw stayed at home knowing there was no chance to attempt to get around Land's End. We, the crew, had very little peace day or night, except at low water. As each tide rose, the surge of the water even in that entrance brought about by the wildness of the sea in Swansea Bay, kept us busy both in daylight and darkness. The slanting rain seemed never-ending, we were seldom dry. I put out the eight inch towrope leading well ahead – about fifteen fathoms, with the other end on another bollard acting as a backspring and from aft put out all the other heavy ropes we had; but we had to keep setting everything up otherwise she would have ranged about and parted them all. At first I had the towrope fast to the port windlass bitt, but before the first week had passed the continuous ranging back and forth of the heavy vessel strained the bitt so much causing the deck to leak over the port bunks bringing forth howls of justified protest. After this we did not use the bitt, but led the hawser to the foremast making it fast how we could. Every fender we had aboard was ground to pieces, even wooden ones with two lanyards soon split and ground themselves to pulp. Not a very exciting story I am afraid, this account of the Fish Quay. No romance there to thrill any reader, but that was life in the 'vessels' on the coast. Being at sea on a passage was the easiest time of all usually. Depressing events such as the above, especially in winter, were not unfamiliar to most of us. During those times everybody aboard would talk about 'getting a steady job ashore' – and they meant it at the moment of utterance. But immediately the situation changed for the better, so did the state of mind. With the ship bowling along with the wind abeam in balmy weather none of us who loved those old ships would have changed it from choice. It was the internal combustion engine that finally took over from the art of sailing, and made it impossible for those who used the power of the wind to live and compete with the power of the motor.

In the autumn following that unpleasant time beside the Fish Quay, we were bound around the land (Land's End) with a cargo of coal from Newport. The weather was fine with a very light southerly wind off the Cornish coast. Below Trevose Head we found some groundsea which may have been the aftermath of some disturbance in the Western Ocean. The *Mary Jones* motoring gaily on, the speed given her by the engine, filling her sails and keeping her booms steady with the little wind there was. About a mile or two past Godrevy Island – we were probably about three miles off the lighthouse – we heard a tremendous clatter from the engine room. I was at the wheel at the time, talking with Captain Billy, who was sat on the skylight. 'That's a bearing gone,' he said. Of course the engine was immediately stopped, an inspection plate taken off and sure enough one of the bearings, made of white metal had melted away. 'Tell Mick to hurry on the dinner,' said the captain. 'She'll be cooled down by the time we've had it. I shall need the fire anyway.' In answer to my look of enquiry he said, 'We shall have to take the head off and get the piston out, I've got to cast another bearing.'

Meantime, as soon as the way was off the ship and the light wind having no effect at all as a steadying 'agent' to the sails, the old ship started to roll in a most uncomfortable manner. The three gaffs aloft, swinging about wildly with every twist and roll, left us with no alternative but to lower the sails down. In any case the mizzen would have had to be taken down because the mizzen throat halyards were the most convenient tackle with which to lift off the engine head – the mizzen mast was just forward of the engine room bulkhead.

None of us enjoyed our dinner in the cabin that day; the ground-sea seemed to lift us and twist us, until we wondered which way next, for the old ship swung about, her head sampling and rejecting every quarter point of the tell-tale compass, which we were all able to see through the cabin skylight.

Capt Shaw produced from a drawer in the engine room a brass mould in two parts bolted together. I then discovered this was not the first time the old Bolinder had run a bearing. Next came a small steel plate which was drilled for the purpose of screwing it to the deck near the sliding door of the galley.

Time now to see about lifting the head off the engine. With the glazed teak lights of the skylight tilted back this was easy except for the rolling, even with three men handling it as it was lifted it was a nightmare until it reached the deck. Then with an eye bolt screwed into the piston head to take the shackle of the tackle it was necessary to put the fall of the tackle on the winch and let one man heave whilst the captain and I 'jagged' it out half an inch at a time.

After this came the ladle on the cabin range and the bubbling of the 'white metal' therein – if only the old vessel would stay still just for a few minutes! But Billy Shaw if he was worried did not show it. I admired him that day on the rolling deck, where everything had to be wedged to keep it still. He poured the liquid metal into the mould, some spilled over the steel plate, but no matter there was some to spare in the ladle: the captain looked up and smiled as I gave a sigh of relief. However, we were not yet out of the wood; the compass told us we were much nearer the line of the bay between the headlands – St Ives Bay. The groundsea was 'lurching' us towards the bay and there was little we could do about it. No anchors would ever have held us had we been driven into St Ives Bay. The bearing cooled, Captain Billy filed it and scraped it, fitted it and scraped it again. Then came the trial run. The piston with the carbon scraped off it slipped into the cylinder – about nine or ten inches in diameter. We fitted the cylinder head. The air bottle was full, and, for once the engine started first time.

Capt Shaw only ran her for a short while, in which time we engaged the air pump to top up the dreaded air bottle – and I headed the vessel out to sea! Then it was necessary to stop the engine, take off the head again, and withdraw the piston just enough to replace the bearings – a few more scrapes on the, evidently, tight parts and everything was assembled again.

Then, blessed relief, the old Bolinder roared into life once again at the first pull of the air lever. No need to urge anybody on to set all sail as quickly as possible, most of our stomachs were 'queasy' after about four hours of unpredictable lurches.

We put the 'kicking straps' on the booms (actually tackles to prevent the booms from swinging inboard when the wind was not sufficient to hold them to leeward) for at that time our engine speed was not enough to produce a breeze strong enough to hold the booms steady in such a groundsea.

After that anxious four hours the thump thump of that old Dutch engine brought joy to our hearts. Roaring out as the ship's stern rose on a swell, the vibration more noticeable with, I suppose, the screw nearer the surface; then sighing, as it were, into a lower key as the stern buried itself into the oily trough. That evening as we steered a course well off shore down towards Pendeen light, what ever sound that old engine made would have been music—pure music! MUSIC — PURE MUSIC!

'Ted,' said Billy Shaw (we had become very good friends by that time), 'as soon as we get to Guernsey', for that was where we were bound, 'we'll take that bearing out again just to make sure.' Some months later, not long before the *Mary Jones* was sold, I left her at Plymouth after discharging a cargo of oats from Ireland. The bearing had never been taken out, and had not given us any trouble. The captain said it was the first time – that uncomfortable time off St Ives Bay – the engine had broken down whilst the ship was on passage.

If this account of the *Mary Jones* speaks more about the engine than about the sails, it is because the engine predominated. That vessel had a deep draught – I believe it was twelve feet loaded – so without the engine she could not have survived for as long as she did. Too big to be chartered for small ports and harbours with shallow water, she had to compete with the many new motor vessels then appearing on the coast, many of them Dutch.

Head winds or fair winds, Billy Shaw kept the engine running. As before stated the *Mary Jones* had a square sail yard, but it was very rarely used because, with the Bolinder thumping away, the advantage gained by the labour of setting the sail on the short passages was negligible.

I left that old but sturdy vessel because I was always poor! As I have said Capt Shaw and myself became good friends, even though he was 20 years older than I was. He knew a lot of people, and other ship masters, and there were many social occasions. In port with the vessel safely beside a quay – but only then – we would go ashore together. My mate's pay of eight pounds per month (30 days) was not adequate, I was always 'over-drawn'. I just had to get out. I thought *this time* I had finished with the vessels. It was about a month later a telegram arrived at my home in Kingston Seymour, it was from the firm of ship brokers who did the business of the *Mary Jones* at Plymouth. 'Could I join the *Two Sisters* at Par as mate?' I could not resist the call, my answer was 'Yes. Will join her tomorrow.' I *believe* it was less than a year later the *Mary Jones* was lost on the Goodwin Sands.

Double topsail schooner
in the English Channel

I remember well one bright September morning in the year 1930 when we left the Cornish port of Par in the schooner *Two Sisters* bound for Boulogne with a cargo of china clay. At the time of sailing the wind was westerly, but as we ran up the English Channel it veered to the north west and became strong and blusterous. However, this was a smooth water wind, and by mid-day the following day we were abreast of the Isle of Wight.

The *Two Sisters* was a double topsail schooner, two-masted, and her overall length from stem to stern was about 95 feet. She was one of the few sailing vessels then left that had not suffered the alleged improvement of having an auxiliary engine installed. She did not even have a motor winch, which was rather unusual even in 1930. Capt Cocks, her master and owner, belonged to the old school and did not take kindly to engines, and his line of thought coincided with my own. I felt I was fortunate to be the mate of a vessel that was still rigged as her 19th century builders had intended her to be. Her cabin was roomy and well appointed. Panelled out with Burma teak, the locker doors and panels were cut to the line of the sheer of the ship, giving the whole a very pleasing appearance, especially when the brass oil lamp, swung in gimbals, was lit at night, for this brought out the mellow beauty of the grain of the wood. Added to this was the movement of the shadows as they flicked and darted about with the movement of the ship whilst the lamp retained its equilibrium.

Off the cabin were two rooms, or cubicles; one to starboard for the captain, the other to port for the mate. This was our sleeping quarters and a very welcome privacy. Had an auxiliary been installed in the vessel, the beauty of the cabin would have vanished, for the engine would have taken up more than half the space and the remainder altered accordingly – with matchboard no doubt.

Another exciting feature of the *Two Sisters* was the fact that her double topsails were still necessary. Had an auxiliary been installed these would almost certainly have been dispensed with, and her bowsprit shortened to give her the proper balance.

Yes, that morning the *Two Sisters*, with the wind abeam, really surged along, the strong but not consistent north-wester causing the rigging to drone, rising to a high pitched hum as the gusts came whistling off the shore. A really exciting sail, the only power the wind. Later we had to take in the upper topsail and the flying jib. Capt Cocks was a prudent master, he saw no sense in carrying away valuable gear just to gain a few miles.

I had never been in a Cornish vessel before, and that forenoon while running up the English Channel I looked into the galley where the cook, a St Austell man, was cooking the dinner. On the cooking range there was an enormous cast-iron oval cooking pot, a stock pot, the cover floating on a 'head of steam' as it lifted to allow the pressure to escape. In the pot there was a plum duff in a basin with a cloth tied around the top; this had been put in first to allow it to boil an hour or more longer than the other commodities. Next (so said the cook) he had put in a huge chunk of salt beef. At a given time later he had put in sliced-up swedes, again later a cabbage, and last of all some potatoes which had been scrubbed but not peeled. I voiced my concern that a raisin pudding should be boiled in the same water as the salt beef, but he assured me that the suet in the pudding would allow no salt water to penetrate; the salt from the beef, he said, was sufficient to flavour the vegetables. This proved to be true, the vegetables had a most delicious flavour, and never have I enjoyed better dinners than those aboard the *Two Sisters*.

In contrast to the Bristol Channel, especially the upper part of it, the English Channel for shallow draught vessels is a lovely stretch of open water. The afternoon of the second day out of Par brought us off Dungeness. But with the blusterly north-wester still persisting, Capt Cocks was loath to leave the weather shore and take his vessel down to a lee shore in such a wind. One could imagine what the sea would have been like off Boulogne. The captain's final decision was to try to get into Dover Harbour. 'This weather could go on for days', he said.

I cannot recall after all these years the exact point of the compass from which the wind was blowing, or the angle of the entrance in relation to the wind. But I certainly remember it was not a favourable wind. The *Two Sisters* would not fetch into the harbour. Capt Cocks, however, was a very competent seaman. He knew his ship and what to expect of her. The first attempt was a long way out, we could all see we were not going to 'make it', but there were three forecastle hands aboard, making us a crew of five and enabling us to put the vessel about smoothly and speedily. The second attempt was more encouraging but we were still too far off the windward pier without enough speed to allow the vessel to be shot up into the wind and so carry her way into the harbour. So it was 'Lee-ho' again, the captain looking somewhat anxious but very determined. We all experienced a splendid lesson in sailing that day off the Dover entrance. The master had the unenviable task of judging by the vessel's speed and leeway whether or not his ship was going to shoot in head to wind through the gap with way enough to carry her clear of the entrance, and still have way enough necessary to manoeuvre her to her anchorage.

The third attempt was again a failure, for the wind veered in a sudden gust making it necessary for the master to put the helm down quickly to avoid getting foul of the leeward pier – I think it was called a breakwater. Round the little ship came again, her jib sheets threshing, the chains attached to the clews being flung about, rattling and beating in the most awesome manner, and woe betide the man who was caught by one of those terrible flails. Added to this the slapping and banging of the heavy canvas in the sails themselves made an indescribable din. Then the booms of the mainsail and the foresail as the vessel was head to wind joined in the fun, swinging back and forth across the deck with the motion of the ship. The heavy sheet blocks, for a few moments free of all restraint, slammed and shook the noisiest of all. Everything shook, the masts, the rigging, the yards – everything; but only for a minute of time. As soon as the vessel's head was past the eye of the wind the jib sheets were hauled in and made fast as tightly as possible before the sails really filled, otherwise they could not have been got in.

By this time the lower topsail was aback (as stated above, the upper topsail had been taken in) pushing the vessel's head around; no time to lose! We were ready at the braces before the call came from the captain. 'Haul lee fore brace!' You see, the brace which had been the weather brace on the other tack had now become the lee brace with the wind on the fore side of the sail. In a strong wind, as we had, two or three hands were needed to haul the yard around quickly, but it was only a short haul, for immediately the wind got behind the now weather leach of the topsail the wind took control, the man on the weather brace preventing the yard from flying around too quickly and therefore doing damage to the gear aloft by surging the fall of the brace with a turn on the belaying pin. This exercise of 'going about' in a small schooner took only about two minutes or a little more to complete (it has taken much longer to describe!) then all was quite again as the vessel steadied up, lying over as all her sails filled and surging ahead like a thing alive. This time, the fourth time, the captain took the vessel farther off, probably about five cables. He had the measure of the tide now and knew what to expect. It was speed he wanted. Came the call 'Lee-ho' for the sixth time – really strenuous work in so short a time – our little ship came about again and filled away for the fourth attempt to get into the harbour. This time the wind increased, lying the old ship over, the high-pitched hum aloft telling its story, and with every sail pulling its best we really stormed along, her head this time pointing well below the pier (or break-water?). Nearing the pier we seemed perilously close to the masonry; we had the topsail clewlines off the pins so that the topsail could be clewed up quickly as soon as the weather leach of the sail started to lift when the ship was brought up into the wind, likewise of course the topsail sheets. We seemed to fly past the end of the pier; here was speed indeed. At that moment the helm was put down, the masts became upright, the headsails slamming and thundering as they spilled out the wind. Watching the weather leach of the topsail I saw it beginning to shiver; a gesture of the hand was sufficient, the two sheets were eased off and the clews hauled up thus enabling the vessel to forge ahead right into the eye of the wind. No need to haul up the buntlines. In no time at all we were through the entrance. The ship still answered her helm, her head paid off, her sails filled and in very little time the captain brought her to in his chosen spot to anchor. With the topsail aback, even though it was still clewed up, we were soon making stern way and at that moment, *the right moment*, came the welcome call 'Let go the anchor'.

Two men went aloft to stow the topsail, while the rest of us lowered and tied up the fore and aft sails. After such plentiful exercise – we had put the ship about seven times in not much over an hour – we were all ravenously hungry and somewhat weary. But the cook would soon be calling us to a meal for hungry men, and we had a quiet night to look forward to; everybody was happy including the master.

The cook, who was over 50 years old, had prepared our meal during the time we were trying to make the harbour. He had been

with Capt Cocks for years and was the real boss in the galley. He
was exempt from most of the other work always to be done on
ship-board. But when the vessel was at sea and his help was needed
with the heavy sails, especially when shortening sail or going about
in turbulent weather, or beating into harbour as we had just done,
he was expected to lend a hand and seldom had to be called to do
so; that was the way of life in the vessels on the coast. It was
seldom a work-shy person was found in a crew, for the very reason
he would not be tolerated, he *could not* be tolerated with so much
heavy work to be done with such few hands; therefore contentment
prevailed – but, of course, everybody grumbled!

The meals, by the way, were also partaken of in the cabin, the
captain and mate sitting at the after end of the table with their
backs to the panelling. Some vessels had tell-tale compasses and
from that position abaft the table the captain was able to see the
lower face of the compass through the glass of the skylight – we
could do so in the schooner *Mary Jones*. But I digress. When the
meal was put on the cabin table by the cook, the master served
himself first, then the mate, the able seamen next and the cook last.
This was the general rule in most of the coasting schooners and
ketches. There was no class distinction about it, just the necessary
mild discipline to ensure some semblance of order. Everybody was
happy.

That particular meal, however, was not very comfortable, the
Two Sisters rolled and tumbled about from the time we let go the
anchor until we left two days later. Although the wind was off the
shore the ship rolled her scuppers under with no let up whatever.
Such disturbance is not unusual in Dover Harbour.

Leaving that harbour as soon as the wind was favourable we
quickly covered the thirty miles or so to Boulogne. I recall we
backed our topsails off the French coast and sent two men in the
ship's boat to make a heavy warp fast to a buoy evidently provided
for such purpose for vessels such as ours.

When the tide was right a pilot came off and took us in to our
berth. He was an elderly man and had been over half a century in
sail. He need not have told us that, for he was a real professional,
sailing us in and berthing the ship beside the quay hardly flattening
a fender. This I recall very clearly but, except that we had a free
discharge, my recollections of Boulogne are extremely vague. One
very vivid recollection however, but hardly relevant to this account,
was that on the quay we saw for the first time ever a lorry with a
hydraulic tipping gear. There must have been some in England, but
we had never seen one.

Leaving Boulogne one evening later, and arriving in the mouth of the Thames the next morning – where we were to load cement at Greenhythe for Falmouth – we saw a number of flags flying at half mast. We learned from the Customs launch which came to speak to us, for we were flying the ensign at the main peak, that the airship the R.101 had struck a hill near Boulogne during the night, a disaster that ended the lives of so many people, hence the flags at half mast. You see we had no radio, or wireless as we called it aboard the *Two Sisters*; we did not want it. It was not even thought about!

That morning before we reached the Thames, although we had a romping off-shore wind through The Downs, lying our light ship over, bustling her along, after we were clear of the North Foreland we had to haul our wind, for Sheerness, where we purposed to anchor, was dead to windward. This meant beating to windward for over thirty miles, and mainly short tacks with a light ship so that, instead of just thirty miles, our old ship with the lee-way she made travelled more than double that distance through the water. With three jib sheets and the staysail bowline to be passed over and hauled taut every time we went about, in addition to having to haul round the heavy yards some times every few minutes, for there were quite a few sailing barges and other traffic about, we had quite a few hours with plenty of exercise with very little let-up.

The Thames sailing barges when loaded appeared to us to be nearly awash. Some loaded with hay stacked so high that the huge loose-footed mainsail had to be brailed up otherwise it would have fouled the bales of hay. But they had enormous square-headed topsails set over the sprit, and their staysails in some cases were so low on the foredeck we imagined the helmsman could never see any craft that may be approaching under their lee bow. Then their bowsprits, very slender and long were bowsed down with the bobstays, in some, so much that they seemed to be pointing down towards the water – like enormous spears. Each of these bowsprits carried one huge jib set on a stay attached to the topmast head; the pulling power of those jibs must have been immense, each, I should imagine, equal to a pair of mighty shire horses! Capt Cocks had been trading to the London river for years; he would not take any chances with the barges. If we were on opposite tacks and the barge was on the port tack (when two sailing vessels are meeting on opposite tacks, the law of the sea is that the ship on the port tack shall always give way to the other) Capt Cocks would always take avoiding action in plenty of time. He reasoned that with the huge stacks of timber and bales of hay piled high above the hatchways carried by some of the barges, coupled with the fact that the foot of the staysail on some was so near to the foredeck thus limiting the view of the crew, and usually there were only two men aboard, there was always the risk of their not seeing the other vessel in time.

One would see a man run up a ladder, run forward over the hay bales, or timber, then down another ladder to the fore deck to attend to his duties. Often the men would have straps around their legs just below the knees, and red handkerchiefs around their necks – like the navvies who used to work for my father on the sea walls at home in the West Country – and this may have had some psychological effect, leading strangers to doubt their nautical ability.

Yes, that morning thrashing to windward in the *Two Sisters* towards Sheerness one had to agree with the captain's caution with regard to the sailing barges. It looked to be dangerous – especially the spear-like bowsprits. Later however I came to know that those fears were groundless. Those barge masters were able and clever mariners, their skills acquired over many generations; their's was a special kind of seafaring, like the trowmen of the River Severn only more so.

A coasting schooner crew could handle a Severn trow, but I doubt if they could have handled a Thames sailing barge.

In due course we loaded the cargo of cement at Greenhythe and came back down the Thames to anchor again at Sheerness. The weather was very inclement with strong south westerly and westerly winds day following day. After just over a week there was a period when I thought we should have left, and as it turned out *we should* have made it to Falmouth; but Capt Cocks did not agree; he reminded me it was 'equinox time' and that it was 175 miles to Ryde Roads, our first really safe anchorage should the heavy southwester return. The captain hoped for a north west wind to carry us to Falmouth. But he was right to be cautious; with an elderly vessel loaded with cement, any straining in heavy weather could have started some deck leaks, and a small amount of water would have ruined a lot of the cargo.

It was the last week in October before we left Sheerness. During that long stay however we, the crew, found plenty to do. Although our ship's masts were bright and clean, it must have been a long time since her yards were scraped and oiled; they were black and hard. The two able seamen and myself oiled (to soften the grime) and scraped, with steel scrapers, every square inch of them; not a very thankful job in blustery weather, but the finished appearance of those three yards, the grain of the pitchpine brought out by the oil, was more than enough reward for our labours. At no time did I ever find a ship where there were no jobs urgently waiting to be done.

We had to beat out from our anchorage, but being loaded and on the ebb tide it was not long before we rounded the North Foreland. But this gave us a beam wind through The Downs and a fair wind down the English Channel.

By the evening of the second day, we had left Sheerness early the morning before, we could see the Isle of Wight, but our fair wind was dying away and it was low water. Added to this an ominous ground-sea was getting up, heaving in from the south west; what bit of wind we had was being rolled out of our sails. Time to put the 'kicking straps' on the booms. We *called them kicking straps*, actually they were preventer tackles attached to heavy strops on the most convenient place on the booms, and hooked to eye bolts in the deck near the bulwarks, the falls of the tackles being made fast to pins in the main rail.

The tackles were made up of one three-fold block and one two-fold rove off with a three inch fall, or more. These prevented the booms from swinging wildly across the deck, in a most unpleasant manner in a heavy ground-sea with little or no wind to fill her sails.

The ground-sea increased with the flood tide; great smooth heaving masses of water came riding in from the south west indicating really bad weather not very far away.

Had our fair wind lasted another hour or two we should have just about managed to get into Ryde Roads. As it was we were caught in the position that Capt Cocks had so carefully tried to avoid.

Before darkness fell we lowered the upper topsail. Going aloft to help tie up the sail, and to make sure that all was as safe as could be for the coming night, the heavy rolling of the vessel with no wind in her sails to steady her caused the yard to swing, rear and jerk in a most frightening manner; we were certainly glad to get in off the dancing footrope, had there been wind to fill the sails and so steady the ship we could have kept our foothold, but that sort of rolling to us high aloft was a nightmare. Yet men did it every day in topsail schooners when experiencing such weather. It was part of the job.

Down on deck Capt Cocks said he had felt some puffs of wind from the west. Bearings taken of the lights ashore showed we were already drifting up channel; no hope now of getting into the back of the Isle of Wight.

We decided to put a couple of rolls in the mainsail (in earlier days before patent reefing gear was invented the canvas itself was rolled up and tied with hempen line with reef knots; in our ship the boom itself was wound around with 'worm' gearing winding the sail with it, thus reducing the area of canvas) thinking the wind may suddenly come upon us; but we had plenty of warning.

Soon the sails filled, the vessel's head payed off and we headed up channel with the wind on the starboard quarter, really thankful to have steerage way and feel the pressure on the helm.

The wind freshened, humming through the rigging; the steadying effect of this on the motion of our little ship was a blessed relief. Although she was lifting her stern and lurched to windward as the wind increased, the uncontrolled rolling was gone.

As soon as the vessel's head was on her course up channel, the captain told the cook to prepare a hot supper of salt beef, potatoes and the inevitable swedes – these being the roots that kept well aboard a vessel – to prepare us all for the night ahead.

Meanwhile the ground-sea that before had been heaving around us smooth and oily, now became seas with white crests that swept hissing past in the darkness, lit as they rose astern by the rays of the stern light. This light was an oil-burning lamp showing a white beam over an arc of the horizon of twelve points. Like our other navigation lights it was constructed of heavy copper, and had to be trimmed and topped up with oil every day – one of the duties of the cook.

We took a couple of rolls in the fore and aft foresail, and soon after another three rolls in the mainsail, for the wind was rapidly increasing. Looking astern the phosphorescence caused by our movement through the water lit up, like liquid fire, the valleys and the crests, telling us how small was the ship.

But the *Two Sisters* had a good robust stern, and aft of the wheel there was a whale-backed deck house that gave some shelter from the wind for the man at the wheel. It also blocked his view directly astern which, in weather such as we experienced that night, was an advantage. Even an experienced and hardened seaman should he, with a quick glance over his shoulder, see a wall of water topped with white rearing menacingly high astern would be apt to duck at such an awesome spectacle, and this just at the moment when the helm needed the most attention.

Taking it in turns, Capt Cocks and two others first, we had all finished supper by the time we passed the Owers lightship. The weather had been worsening all the time, increasing the sea, the music of the wind in the cordage and rigging now too high-pitched to be pleasant. The *Two Sisters* was proving, to me anyway, to be quite an able vessel in such a situation. However, when an extra heavy sea came roaring up astern, its crest breaking and foaming white as it lifted and buried our stern, one had to be ready to catch her with the helm, for such a mighty onrush of water had a tendency to screw the vessel's stern around, thus exposing the weather side to the next following monster. If this should happen (such an incident is known as broaching to) the decks could be swept clear of everything, her hatchways probably stove in by such overwhelming power, and founder in a matter of minutes.

One thing I was most thankful for during that rather anxious night was the lower topsail. The pulling power of that sail in a schooner is tremendous. Made of top grade No. 1 canvas it had stout chain sheets, and was made to withstand such weather us we had; without it I doubt if we should have made it up the Channel that night.

In the trough of the seas our fore and aft foresail and the mainsail, reefed down as they were, would on occasion for a moment or two actually loose the wind, causing the sails to slat. But the lower topsail was up there always full, pulling and dragging the ship along.

It was this slatting as mentioned above that was the cause of the fore staysail splitting from head to foot about halfway through the night not far below Beachy Head. With the ship's head deep in a trough, the sail would sometimes loose the wind, then, as the bow reared high on the crest of an overtaking comber the sail would fill with a bang – a loud bang. The jibs, being shorter in the foot, could be sheeted harder in and did not give so much trouble.

I must mention here that all of us stayed on deck that night after supper, most of the time in what bit of shelter there was the foreside of the deckhouse aft. Both companion ways of the forecastle and the cabin were made as secure as possible with the slides in, and the whaleback tops pulled over and fastened.

The cook, however, popped down occasionally to bank up the fires. Of course there was the galley abaft the foremast where the cook spent most of his time that night, but ready at all times to turn out if necessary, also to brew tea or cocoa if required. The other hands too took turns in that doubtful harbour of refuge.

I spent a lot of time at the wheel that night. Capt Cocks, then an elderly man, I belief suffered from a hernia, for during the first hour of the run back up channel when he was at the helm, whilst we attended to other things, and the vessel was becoming somewhat hard to steer, he looked to be drawn and distressed. Yet whenever I had occasion to leave the helm he was always ready to take over. I suspected that had he been able he would have stayed at the helm all night. Such is a man's love for his ship.

When the staysail split, however, something had to be done about it quickly. I took two hands, including the cook from St Austell for he had stowed it away, opened up the hatch and dragged the spare staysail up from the sail locker.

Before this, by the light of the anchor light which the cook had prepared and lit in the galley, we had lowered the split sail and cut it away from the hanks on the fore stay. The simple way to bend on any headsail – usually of course, done in harbour – is to shackle on the tack, then the halyards to the head, then seize on the hanks as the sail is hoisted up the stay. But that night we had to do everything before the sail was hoisted. We seized the lower hanks on first – about twenty two of them – together with the tack, clew and bowline, then waiting our chance in a trough of the sea we set the sail. We got very wet while on the fore deck, some of the overtaking seas, cleft in two, as it were, as our stern rose high would topple aboard in the waist of the ship and come sluicing down to the foredeck, swirling knee deep around the windlass, white and cold.

Back on the quarter deck the captain looked as if he was in pain again. During the time the ship was without her staysail she naturally carried more weather helm, and was therefore considerably harder to steer. But he insisted I put on dry clothes before I relieved him. Should the reader wonder why one of the able seamen was not put at the helm during that night, the answer is not that they were not capable of steering the ship even in hard and blusterous weather, but that was an extra heavy gale with an unusually heavy sea, in which anything could have happened at any minute; prudence demanded that the men were ready at any minute to act quickly to attend to any gear that may have carried away, and this included going aloft or forward to the bowsprit. Their reactions would not have been one hundred per cent after a spell at the old ship's kicking wheel.

The captain was sitting muffled on the cabin skylight, a shadowy figure in the dim light filtering through the slits not covered by the canvas hood, from the cabin lamp below. I could imagine his thoughts and his anxiety, having got so far down channel, and so near to Ryde Roads, and then having to run all the way back up channel; his ship and her gear taking such a hammering that the cost to repair could easily eat up all the meagre freight her cargo would bring.

I say meagre because it was so, the reason being so many smart motorized Dutch coasters were appearing on our coasts, drawing less water than the *Two Sisters*, and some carrying three times the amount of cargo; they were subsidized by the Dutch government. They were able to run to schedule except in very bad weather and were consequently popular with the brokers. The beautiful little schooners that had graced our coasts for so many generations, were being slowly but relentlessly put out of business.

That night at the kicking wheel of the *Two Sisters* as she was driven up the English Channel before the storm, I was forced to accept the hitherto unacceptable fact, that, even with the auxiliary engines installed, the day of the sailing coasters were numbered.

In the early hours of the morning, although the force of the wind had not increased, the sea became more erratic. We all had some very anxious moments when our vessel's stern would twist away to leeward as if thrown aside by those mighty forces that came marching from the south west. It was then that an extra hand was needed at the wheel to give the ship all the weather helm one could. No need to call, the help was always there, ready and willing.

With the coming of daylight we were within sight of the cliffs of Dover, but they were not much whiter than the sea around us. Seeing in broad daylight that wild seascape of moving hills and valleys, we felt justly proud of the old ship that had stood up so well to such a display of wrath the elements had given us during that anxious night.

We were, of course, making for The Downs, that ancient anchorage that had accommodated all kinds of ships from westerly and south westerly gales for centuries.

Leaving Dover astern and on our port quarter, it would soon be time to change our course to get into The Downs, and this meant we should have to jibe – not a very pleasant undertaking in such weather and heavy sea. However we made what preparation we could, which was little except haul the booms of the mainsail and foresail in as far as was prudent before the actual jibe took place, thus shortening the distance the booms would have to swing across when the vessel's stern passed through the eye of the wind.

The sea as if to spite our efforts seemed to be steeper and more nasty than ever, probably owing to the narrower waters of the straits. Neither did the wind relent even for a short while.

Capt Cocks now took the helm. Myself and two others stood ready by the mainsheet, the other hand by the fore sheet. Standing where I was I could watch the sea astern, for we needed and hoped for a less turbulent patch.

We could not delay much longer otherwise we should be edging off the shore, and the Goodwin Sands were not far to leeward.

The captain looking across at me called: 'It'll have to be soon!' and to my 'It just as well be now' replied: 'Stand by then!' and put the helm hard to starboard. No need to tell the crew to take in every bit of sheet they could as the sails lost the wind, everybody knew to do so was vital. I watched the vessel's head swing a couple of points to port, falling away from a passing sea. The booms down to port with the roll of the ship, resisted all our efforts to haul them aboard during those vital moments when the stern was in the wind's eye. Then, as the vessel rolled back to starboard, we frantically hauled in as much sheet as we could, but we were not quick enough. Immediately the full weight of the wind got behind the sail the heavy main boom swung across with a crash like thunder, tearing the four inch fall from our hands even though we had a turn on the cleat.

The 38-foot boom, some 10½ inches in diameter whipped as if it was made of cane; simultaneously, the boom dropped and we saw the main rigging slacken.

Looking aloft we could see that the jumper stay had parted; this was a calamity. The jumper stay was a wire stay about one inch in diameter. Leading from the foremast head to the mainmast head, it held the two masts in their positions the right distance apart, whilst the forestay leading down to the stem and the main rigging leading aft, and set up with hempen lanyards (not *rigging screws* in those days) ensured a fore and aft rigidity. However, without a jumper stay all tautness was gone.

To add to the confusion, the braces, which controlled and swung the topsail yards, were not attached to the mainmast any more, but had broken free and were hanging from the yardarms.

Although this has taken a long time to describe, it must have happened in *less than two minutes*; brought about by being forced to jibe in such a vicious sea and ferocious weather. It was discovered later that the jumper stay itself had *not* parted, but the huge shackle made of ⅞" mild steel that secured the stay to the eyebolt in the masthead had been torn apart. Into that massive shackle had been shackled the smaller ones attached to the blocks of the braces of the two upper yards (but this rather doubtful arrangement had been done before my time in the ship).

Immediately after the gear aloft had carried away, thus allowing the mainmast to spring back towards the stern loaded as it was by the heavy mainsail, and the boom and gaff; that movement brought the heavy boom down to within very little clearance of the gallant rail of the bulwarks. Two of us quickly took the burton (a long tackle used for launching the boat) that was attached to the main-mast head and managed to rig it with a long improvised strop to the foot of the foremast, and this allowed us to set the mast up a little and enabled us to use the topping lift to keep the boom clear of the deck-house aft. But the burton was only a very temporary measure; it would have to be released if the foresail boom should have to cross the deck.

Meanwhile the other two hands had managed to get hold of the falls of the braces, let draw the bowline and pass over the jib sheets, and this was about all we could do. But the ship looked a sorry mess; the jib stays slack, curving out to leeward; the lovely pitch-pine mainmast leaning aft, wobbling, the most frightening of all. All this, which I have taken so long to describe, happened in a very few minutes of time.

Nevertheless, we were round and heading towards The Downs. Had the mast gone by the board we could easily have ended up on the dreaded Goodwin Sands.

I had just taken the helm from the captain to give him a short spell before we were able to prepare to anchor in The Downs, when one of the crew called out that he had seen a lifeboat. Looking to leeward when our stern rose high, sure enough, about three cables distant, we saw a lifeboat's bow seemingly to point to the clouds, and then dive, a flash of blue into a moving valley – a valley of white.

We thought they must be going to, or looking for, some other craft, but when we again saw them they seemed to be heading towards us. Before long the lifeboat was about a cables length away under our lee, rearing and plunging, an exciting picture even to our red and weary eyes. Capt Cocks fearing salvage, waved them away, shouting to say we were alright, but in that wild commotion he just as well to have shouted at the moon. He also cautioned the crew not to attempt to take a rope should they try to come up under our quarter and offer one. I cannot recall what lifeboat it was, but at the time the captain referred to them as 'those fellows from Deal!' Whatever the captain's feelings may have been we, the crew, were certainly glad to see them, their very presence gave us some uplift for we were desperately tired. I suppose even now there is somewhere a record of the launching of the lifeboat, and from which harbour it came. She may have been called out thinking we were likely to be lost on the Goodwins.

I have always felt somewhat guilty of the casual way the lifeboat was treated, with never an inquiry afterwards from our ship about the affair.

Well, it was not long before we were in smoother water, and found some relief from the howling wind in the shelter of the weather shore. The lifeboat had by then disappeared, whither we did not know.

What a blessed relief it was to come to anchor, even though the vessel still tumbled about, and have a solid meal in peace.

Before anybody could turn in, however, the jumper stay had to be properly set up again. We quickly rigged a gantline from the cap of the mainmast and hauled up the heavy wire; then with a handy block and tackle between strops on the stay and the masthead bowsed the two together and shackled the stay in its place.

Then, of course, the lanyards of the main rigging had to be set up, likewise the fore rigging. Although many minor things had yet to be attended to and repaired, they could wait for, if necessary owing to a change of wind, we could leave The Downs at any time. Time now for what we craved most of all, the solace of sleep.

Capt Cocks had managed a few hours in his bunk whilst we were fixing the jumper stay and setting up the rigging. He now kept anchor watch, this mainly in the galley by the fire – this was usual, as long as one was on deck and awake.

The wind eased the next day towards evening, and by daylight the following morning came from the eastward, so we hove up the anchor and sailed around to Dover Harbour. Here we were able to give attention to the many things that needed to be put right before we proceeded on our way. The captain was put ashore in the boat to send the usual telegram home, taking our letters with him.

Being unable to make Ryde Roads when we ran into the bad weather during our run down the Channel, had added nearly 300 miles to the distance we had to travel from the Thames to Falmouth Harbour. Twenty years before, this would not have been notice-able, with so many sailing vessels trading around our coasts it occurred too often to be worthy of comment. It could not be avoided. Now, however, the internal combustion engine had changed the scene, and with it the line of thought. Brokers and merchants expected cargoes such as ours to be delivered in a few days and, with the smart and speedy motor craft becoming more numerous, and cutting the freightage, those craft got the charters.

The *Two Sisters* cargo had been in her hold for nearly three weeks, and here we were still at Dover. Not much doubt as to what class of ship would prevail. The *Two Sisters* sailed into Falmouth Harbour about the middle of November. The round trip described had taken just over two months.

The wages due to me for that period of time was under 20 pounds – a sailor's month for some unknown reason was not just four weeks, but 30 days. The mate of a schooner, or a coasting ketch, to be able to keep his job was expected to be able to supervise the loading and stowage of cargo, the discharging of cargo and to move the vessel from berth to berth whether in docks or in a tidal river, for if we docked anywhere within reasonable distance of the master's home, as soon as we touched the quay he would be ashore and away.

Also, the mate had to be able to do – or to show others – any maintenance to sails, gear, or rigging except major repairs. At sea he had to be able to keep a watch both by day and night in coastwise vessels, for obviously the master had to have his watch below. Without knowing the rule of the road at sea, or having elementary knowledge of chart work and navigation he, the mate, could not have done the job. Had he tried, he could not have lasted.

Nevertheless, men, married men, stayed in those old vessels when they could have got better paid jobs in steam. The main reason for this was because they loved their ships, the ships many of their fathers had built and served in; they belonged to a special community with its own environment. To serve in a motor auxiliary vessel had to be accepted. But to go into steam was a step down.

Registration details of the vessels in which the author served

SAILING COASTERS

Annie Christian
ON 76819, schooner, built Barnstaple, 1881, 69 tons, dimensions
76.5 × 20.5 × 9.0 ft. Signal: J.C.F.H.

Date	Port of Registry	Owner	Further Details
1882	Ramsey	Edward Quayie, Ramsey, Isle of Man	
1885	Wigtown	David B Shaw, Garlieston, Wigtown	
1889	Liverpool	Isaac Allen, Watchet	
1894	ditto		Rerigged as ketch
1913	Bridgwater	The Somerset Trading Co Ltd, Bridgwater, Manager, Robert Y Foley	
1917			59 tons
1920	Bridgwater	Leonard M Bowerman (Manager), Bridgwater	
1925	ditto	Cecil Bowerman (Manager)	
1929	Bideford	Philip W Harris, Appledore, Devon	Renamed *Ade*

Broken up at Appledore, 1946. Her fiddlehead was saved and is
now preserved in private hands.

Garlandstone
ON 128746, ketch, built Calstock, 1909, 62 tons, dimensions
76.0 × 20.2 × 9.0 ft.

Date	Port of Registry	Owner	Further Details
1910	Milford	John J D Russan (Manager), Studdulph, Milford Haven, Pembrokeshire	
1913			54 tons
1913	ditto	Address now Musselwick, St Ishmaels, Pembrokeshire	Engine fitted 40 h.p.
1920	ditto	Andrew Murdock (Manager), Gloucester	
1947		Alfred Parkhouse (Manager), Braunton, Devon	
1949			Engine 75 B.H.P.

In 1981 the *Garlandstone*, now owned by the National Museum
of Wales, lay in Porthmadog in Gwynedd under restoration
towards her appearance at the time Mr Eglinton sailed in her.

Jane
ON 26713, ketch, built Runcorn 1800, 33 tons, dimensions 61.8
× 14.5 × 5.2 ft. Signal: P.M.G.T.

Date	Port of Registry	Owner	Further Details
1857	Beaumaris		
1860	Bridgwater		
1866	ditto	W Smart	
1872	ditto		Rig sloop
1876			42 tons
1879	ditto	Henry J Winslade, West St, Bridgwater	
1881			Trow, 44 tons
1882	ditto		Ketch
1890	ditto	Henry G Winslade (Manager), Bridgwater	37 tons
1900	ditto	William Webb (Manager), Pawlett, Somerset	
1901	ditto	Peter Hart, Uphill, Somerset	
1906			40 tons
1919	ditto	Leonard P Smart (Manager), Weston-Super-Mare	

The Port Registry Transcript in the National Maritime Museum gives slightly conflicting information. W Smart bought her from Beaumaris in 1860. On reregistration in 1879 she is shown as a trow of dimensions 66.9 × 40.5 × 4.9 ft. Not until 1901 is she shown again as a ketch. In 1905 her dimensions are again altered to 68.5 × 16.3 × 6.2 ft. She was finally converted to a lighter on 31 December 1925. Subsequently she was hulked at Bristol and was broken up *c.* 1940.

Lily
ON 108020, ketch, built Penryn, 1897, 25 tons, dimensions 56 × 16 × 5.7 ft.

Date	Port of Registry	Owner	Further Details
1897	Falmouth	Phillip Henry Dawe, Penzance, Cornwall and Edward Dixon Anderton, Falmouth	
	ditto	D Kingsland Norton, Topsham, Devon	
1911	ditto	Frederick John Bennett, Ilfracombe	
1916	Barnstaple	Alfred Oxenham, Lynmouth, Devon	
1927	ditto	Lt.-Col. Holman F Stephens, Tonbridge, Kent	Engine fitted 23 tons

Foundered off the River Usk, 9–10 January 1929.

Mary Jones
ON 44050, schooner, built Flint, 1863, 113 tons, dimensions 93.0 × 22.1 × 10.7 ft. Signal: T.R.L.N.

Date	Port of Registry	Owner	Further Details
1864	Chester	William Jones	
1866	ditto	Thomas Williams, Queensferry, Flint	
1875	ditto	William Jones, Queensferry, Flint	
1876			98 tons
1877	ditto	William Jones, Watergate, Chester	

Date	Port	Owner	Further Details
1879	ditto	Thomas Hughes, Connah's Quay, Flint	
1891	ditto	Edward John Peers (Manager), Connah's Quay	
1892			85 tons
1894	ditto	Robert Edwards (Manager), Connah's Quay, Flint	
1900	ditto	Robert Edwards, Connah's Quay, Flint, Walter Reney (Manager), Connah's Quay	
1908			90 tons
1911		Charles A Reney now Manager	
1917	ditto	Arthur Galsworth (Manager), Appledore, Devon	
1923	Bideford		Fitted with engine 60 B.H.P., 73 tons
1925	ditto	Philip K Harris (Manager), Appledore, Devon	
1926	ditto	Marian Trading Co Ltd, London WC2	
1929	ditto	William H Shaw, Newport, Monmouthshire	
1930	ditto	Mrs Anne S Shaw (Manager), Newport, Monmouthshire	
1931	ditto	Evelyn H Jones (Manager), Farnborough, Kent	

Wrecked off Ramsgate, February 1932.

Renown
ON 11939, schooner, built Bideford 1856, 63 tons, dimensions
65.2 × 18.5 × 8.7 ft. Signal: K.V.Q.T.

Date	Port of Registry	Owner	Further Details
1857	Swansea	E Griffiths, Porthcawl	
1861		Evans & Co, Porthcawl	
1867	ditto	John David, Porthcawl, Glamorgan	
1870	ditto	Josiah Evans, New Quay, Cardiganshire	
1886	ditto	Hugh Thomas, Amlwch, Anglesey	
1893			50 tons

1906	ditto	Owen G Owens (Manager), Rhosneigr	
1907	ditto	Thomas Hutchings (Manager), Appledore, Devon	
1916	ditto	Thomas J Hutchings (Manager), Appledore, Devon	Rerigged as ketch

Foundered off Mumbles, 19 June 1926.

Thomasine and Mary
ON 19226, ketch, built Boscastle, 1855, 49 tons, dimensions 55.8 × 18.1 × 8.2 ft. Signal: M.R.C.Q.

Date	Port of Registry	Owner	Further Details
1855	Padstow	Richard Blake Hellyar	
1856	Swansea	George Augustus Munro and others, Swansea	
1858	Bridgwater	William Henry Perkins Hole and Henry George Hole, Watchet, Somerset	
1869	ditto	Henry George Hole, Watchet, Somerset	
1872	ditto		Smack
1878	ditto	Llewellin Hole, Watchet, Somerset	
1900	ditto		Rerigged as ketch
1912	ditto		38 tons
1918	ditto	Mrs Ellen A Lamey (Manager), Appledore, Devon	
1919	ditto	William J Lamey (Manager), Appledore, Devon	

Wrecked at Walton Bay, 7 September 1926.

Two Sisters
ON 84246, schooner, built Bosham, 1882, 115 tons, dimensions 94.8 × 21.8 × 9.7 ft. Signal: H.V.Q.G.

Date	Port of Registry	Owner	Further Details
1884	Portsmouth	Mrs Kate Smart, Bosham	
1908	ditto	Mrs Kate Smart (Manager), Bosham	

1912	Bideford	Joseph Jewell (Manager), Plymouth
1916		100 tons
1918	ditto	The Hook Shipping Co Ltd, Haverfordwest, Pembrokeshire
1920	ditto	Theophilus W Couch (Manager), Pentewan, Cornwall

Broken up at Mylor, Cornwall, 1947.

OCEAN-GOING VESSELS

British Marshal
On 133513 Steel single-screw tanker, built by Tyne Iron SB Co, Willington Quay on Tyne, Wallsend, 1912. 4158 gross tons, 6031 dead weight, dimensions 357.2 × 48.2 × 28.2 ft. Triple-expansion engines by Wallsend Slipway Co Ltd, Wallsend on Tyne. h.p. 363, 10 knots. Signal: H.W.N.T.
   Built as *Russian Prince* for Prince Line Ltd. Transferred to British Tanker Co Ltd, London, 1918. Sold: Societa Italiana Trasporti Petroliferi and renamed *Tritone* for a little under £35,000, November 1929.

Oxonian
ON 109475 Steel single-screw 4-mastered steamer, built by Charles Connell & Co., Glasgow, 1898. 6383 gross tons, dimensions 459.0 × 52.5 × 31.0 ft. Triple-expansion engines by D Rowan & Co 550 h.p. 11 knots. Signal: Q.J.L.R.
   Built as *Pinemore* for Johnston Line Ltd, Liverpool, transferred to F Leyland & Co Ltd, Liverpool, and renamed, 1903. Sold: P and W MacLennan £11,500, for breaking up, May 1928.

Phototypeset by Input Typesetting Ltd., London sw19 8dr
Printed in England for Her Majesty's Stationery Office
by Billing and Sons Limited Guildford, London, Oxford, Worcester
Dd 696320 C 65